Exploring Blazor

Creating Server-side and Client-side Applications in .NET 7

Second Edition

Taurius Litvinavicius

Apress®

Exploring Blazor: Creating Server-side and Client-side Applications in .NET 7

Taurius Litvinavicius
Kaunas, Lithuania

ISBN-13 (pbk): 978-1-4842-8767-5   ISBN-13 (electronic): 978-1-4842-8768-2
https://doi.org/10.1007/978-1-4842-8768-2

Managing Director, Apress Media LLC: Welmoed Spahr
Acquisitions Editor: Smriti Srivastava
Development Editor: Laura Berendson
Coordinating Editor: Shrikant Vishwakarma
Copy Editor: Kim Wimpsett

Cover designed by eStudioCalamar

Cover image by Erik Witsoe on Unsplash (www.unsplash.com)

Distributed to the book trade worldwide by Apress Media, LLC, 1 New York Plaza, New York, NY 10004, U.S.A. Phone 1-800-SPRINGER, fax (201) 348-4505, e-mail orders-ny@springer-sbm.com, or visit www.springeronline.com. Apress Media, LLC is a California LLC and the sole member (owner) is Springer Science + Business Media Finance Inc (SSBM Finance Inc). SSBM Finance Inc is a **Delaware** corporation.

For information on translations, please e-mail booktranslations@springernature.com; for reprint, paperback, or audio rights, please e-mail bookpermissions@springernature.com.

Apress titles may be purchased in bulk for academic, corporate, or promotional use. eBook versions and licenses are also available for most titles. For more information, reference our Print and eBook Bulk Sales web page at www.apress.com/bulk-sales.

Any source code or other supplementary material referenced by the author in this book is available to readers on GitHub (https://github.com/Apress). For more detailed information, please visit www.apress.com/source-code.

Printed on acid-free paper

Table of Contents

About the Author

Taurius Litvinavicius is a businessman and technology expert based in Lithuania who has worked with organizations in building and implementing various projects in software development, sales, and other fields of business. He currently works on modern financial applications and consults for companies on technology and cost-related issues. With most of his projects, he uses cutting-edge and cost-effective technologies, such as Blazor.

About the Technical Reviewer

Fabio Claudio Ferracchiati is a senior consultant and senior analyst/developer using Microsoft technologies. He works for BluArancio (`www.bluarancio.com`). He is a Microsoft Certified Solution Developer for .NET, a Microsoft Certified Application Developer for .NET, a Microsoft Certified Professional, and a prolific author and technical reviewer. Over the past ten years, he's written articles for Italian and international magazines and coauthored more than ten books on a variety of computer topics.

Introduction

For many years the web development community has been waiting for something new to escape the dreaded JavaScript monopoly. Finally, the time has arrived—first with the release of WebAssembly and now with the release of Blazor. This book will explore Blazor in depth, and with that, you will understand what role WebAssembly plays in this tool stack.

To start, you will learn what Blazor is, where it runs, and how to start using it. Blazor is convenient to code and also has tremendous business value. Although the technology is still relatively young, I have already managed and taken part in the development of a large-scale platform—mashdrop.com—and from that experience, can testify as to Blazor's efficiency and ease of use.

This book will focus on practicality and practice; you can expect lots of sample code and some exercises to complete. In fact, you will work through five exercises, covering all types of Blazor, and explore some use cases. I believe in experiential learning, which is why, from the early stages of the book, we will be exploring Blazor by looking at code samples and folder structures of projects. Since Blazor is not a stand-alone technology like a programming language, the best way to learn it is to interact with it, see what it looks like in the code, and uncover some similarities with technologies using the same programming language—in this case C#. You will see, you will do, and most importantly you will learn.

Source Code

All the source code used in this book is available for download at https://github.com/apress/exploring-blazor-2e.

CHAPTER 1

Introduction to Blazor

In this book, you will learn about Blazor, a modern framework for developing web applications using C#. You'll learn about all the features of Blazor, from the most basic to the more advanced. You will learn the fundamentals of Blazor syntax and project setup, as well as exciting modern features such as picking files and accessing them using C# in a web browser, accessing API data using JSON, and using many of the other latest features of Blazor. In addition, I will demonstrate what you can achieve in Blazor and provide a few tasks for you to practice yourself, along with the solutions I created for them.

Before you start, you need to know and prepare a few things. This is not an introductory book to C# or .NET Core development, so you should already have good knowledge of C# and be able to build applications with it. It does not matter if you develop back-end applications, Windows applications, or mobile applications; as long as you use C#, you will find something familiar in Blazor. If you haven't already, you'll need to install Visual Studio 2022 and make sure that you have the .NET 7 SDK installed on your computer.

What Is Blazor?

Blazor is a web UI framework that allows you to use C# and .NET Core on the front end. It allows you to develop your front-end logic in a couple of different ways using the C# programming language, which is something that you will explore later in this chapter.

© Taurius Litvinavicius 2023
T. Litvinavicius, *Exploring Blazor*, https://doi.org/10.1007/978-1-4842-8768-2_1

Technical aspects aside, think of it this way: in any standard web development project, you would need to have two people, one for the JavaScript and the other for the back end. Sometimes you also need a designer to work with HTML elements and CSS and do other design-related tasks. The Blazor technology will not remove any dependency for a designer, but it will surely remove the dependency on JavaScript. (However, JavaScript can still be used with the Blazor technology.)

Blazor uses the Razor syntax (C# mixed with HTML), which will be covered in Chapter 2, so any familiarity with the Razor syntax will give you an edge when developing. There are some differences, though, as you will see shortly. Most important, your C# code in Razor (the `.cshtml` file) will execute only when the page is loaded, but in Blazor (the `.razor` file) the code will execute on the loaded page on various events, such as `onclick`, `onchange`, and others.

Blazor uses WebSocket to communicate with the server as well as work on the server side, or it uses the WebAssembly technology, which allows for C# to be built on the client side. This is where the different types of Blazor technology come into play.

What Is WebAssembly?

WebAssembly is a technology that allows you to compile languages such as C++ or C# in the browser, thus allowing Blazor to exist. It first appeared as a minimum viable product in early 2017, and while the technology is still in its early years, it is being co-developed by companies such as Microsoft, Google, Apple, and others. The technology has the support of most major browsers (`https://webassembly.org/roadmap/`)—Edge, Chrome, Firefox, Opera, and Maxthon (MX)—and the equivalent mobile versions. With its growth, we can expect the support to be there for a long time. In general, Blazor simply sends a source code file to the browser, and WebAssembly compiles it into a binary file.

WebAssembly gives you a safe, sandboxed environment, so it appears similarly as running JavaScript. Nothing is accessible from outside the specific browser tab the user is using.

Blazor Types

The *server-side* type of Blazor will run all the logic on the server side, mainly using WebSockets to accomplish tasks (Figure 1-1). Although it does give you an ability to use C# to write the front end, this may not be the most efficient option. You will eliminate the need for API calls with this option, as you will simply inject your libraries directly to the front-end part.

Figure 1-1. *Blazor Server App template in Visual Studio 2022*

The *client* type of Blazor runs completely on the client side, on the browser (Figure 1-2). You will have your pages on the server, but other than that, the client side handles everything. So, this is great for presentation websites or websites that provide calculators and other such services. If you need database interactions or if you already have APIs and class libraries, this will not be your choice.

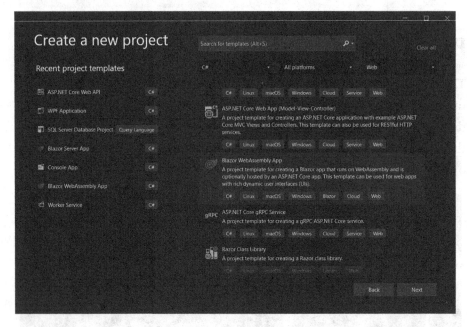

Figure 1-2. *Blazor WebAssembly App template in Visual Studio 2022*

There are also other possible variations of these two types. One of them is Blazor hosted; this project is client-side Blazor (Blazor WebAssembly) interconnected with the web API project. The client Blazor and API program run separately, but development-wise they will be able to share a common code library, mostly for data models. There is also a progressive web application (PWA) option, which allows the Blazor client to run offline. Finally, you can add API capabilities (controllers and such) to a Blazor server project.

Along with these main projects, you will also find a Razor Class Library project (Figure 1-3). This allows you to create Blazor components with all the Blazor features in a code library and if needed publish that to NuGet.

Figure 1-3. *Razor Class Library template in Visual Studio 2022*

Summary

There is no best type of Blazor; as you have seen throughout this chapter, every option has its own use case. Everything depends on what your project needs right now and, more important, what it will need in the future. If you are not sure, simply go with the client-side version, as it will be the most diverse option. In the next chapter, we will dive deeper into Blazor and explore the syntax and some other topics. You will see that while the structure may be different, for the most part, coding happens in the same way for all types of Blazor.

CHAPTER 2

Razor Syntax and the Basics of Blazor

This chapter will get you started with Blazor. As mentioned in the previous chapter, all three types of Blazor have a lot in common. Before we can go any further, we will need to look at the syntax and see how it works. Then we will get into the essentials of Blazor, such as bindings and method execution; all of these topics will be used later in the book.

In this chapter, you will learn about the following:

- Syntax

- Element and variable bindings

- Method executions

- General page events

Differences Between Razor and Blazor

Simplistically speaking, the difference between Razor and Blazor is that Razor will be executed once on page launch, while the Blazor functionality will work all the time. In other words, the loops and logic statements will get re-evaluated in Blazor, while with Razor it will happen only once.

© Taurius Litvinavicius 2023
T. Litvinavicius, *Exploring Blazor*, https://doi.org/10.1007/978-1-4842-8768-2_2

Syntax

As mentioned previously, if you know Razor syntax, you will know Blazor syntax. However, if you do not know Razor syntax, this is the section for you. The Blazor code goes into a markup file named `.razor`, which contains HTML as well as C# code.

Comments

Even though we use HTML syntax in a Blazor file, we do not use HTML comments. Instead, we use Razor syntax and get a beautiful and efficient commenting system, with no comments left on a generated page. Listing 2-1 illustrates this.

Listing 2-1. Razor/Blazor Comment Syntax

```
@*
Below is a test p element
*@

<p>Test paragraph</p>
```

As shown in Listing 2-1, you simply start a comment section with @* and then end with *@. You can also use the standard HTML comments, but using the Razor/Blazor syntax will be easier to see in the code. The Razor/Blazor comment syntax characters get highlighted, and the actual comment is displayed in green. The comments will not be visible in published app using browser developer tools.

Sections

Razor syntax is basically C# and HTML code in one file, and while they do interact, you need some higher contrast between the two languages. That is where all the different sections come in; as you will see, the sections are C# dominant, and they are used to highlight the C# parts of the code.

In Listing 2-2, a variable is being declared, and then it is displayed directly in a paragraph using C# code. So, for a single variable and the construction of classes, you can simply use the @ sign and write everything on a single line. If you want to write more than one line for a variable declaration, you need to create a section using @{ ... }.

Listing 2-2. Basic Blazor Sections

```
@{
string teststring = "tst";
}
<p>@teststring</p>
```

At this point, this may look very simple, so let's dive into a few more examples.

In Listing 2-3, the testint variable is declared and set to the value 0, followed by an if statement checking if the value of testint is not 0. Since the statement criteria is not satisfied, whatever is inside the if statement is not displayed. If the testint variable is set to any other value than 0, say 1, the HTML paragraph tag and value would be displayed. The C# code in the @{ } section is highlighted, and it requires no @ sign for each line. The if statement part starts with the @ sign and creates a section similar to the previous example. This means the HTML code in the if statement section is not highlighted in any way.

Listing 2-3. if Statement Syntax

```
@{
int testing = 0;
}

@if (testint != 0)
{
<p>Is not equal to zero</p>
}
```

In Listing 2-4, a for loop has been created, looping five times. Each loop creates a new paragraph tag containing the value for the current iteration, i. The for loop part is highlighted in a slight shade of gray, while the @ signs are highlighted in yellow. The HTML part inside the loop is not highlighted, but the C# code is; that is how you can tell the difference between HTML markup and C# code.

Listing 2-4. Syntax Coloring

```
@for (int i = 0; I < 5; i++)
{
<p>@i</p>
}
```

Finally, there's the code section (see Listing 2-5) where all the methods should be declared. The binding variables should also be added to the code section, which you will find later in this chapter (in the "Blazor Binds" section).

Listing 2-5. Code Section

```
<p>test</p>
@code {
  int a;
```

```
double b = 2.5;
void testmethod() {
}
}
```

Blazor Binds

Blazor allows you to bind an HTML input value to a variable and vice versa. Therefore, for the most part, we can call all bindings two-way. If you bind a text box (input type text) to a string variable, the displayed value will be the value of that string. Different elements will work differently, and there are many use cases for this.

Binding to an Element

Binding to an element is simple. Not all elements can be bound, but most can.

Elements where values can be bound to a variable are as follows:

- Input (except for file type)

- Textarea

- Select

The listed elements are the most common elements that can be bound, but most others will work in some way.

In Listing 2-6, two simple variables have been declared, and initial have been values assigned. Listing 2-7 shows how to bind them to different elements.

Listing 2-6. Variables

```
@code {
  string teststring = "test value";
  bool testbool = true;
}
```

Listing 2-7. Bindings

```
<input type="checkbox" @bind="@testbool">
<input @bind="@teststring">
<textarea @bind="@teststring"></textarea>
```

In Listing 2-7, a Boolean value is bound to a check box, checked/unchecked, and the same is true for a radio button. The string value can be bound to any text value such as input, textarea, and others. When the input value changes, the variable value changes, and when the variable value changes, the value displayed in the input tag will change too.

The previous option can be considered a default option to do the binding; however, there are additional parameters that you can use.

In Listing 2-8, you can see a binding on a specific event, rather than the default one. In this particular example, you can see that the oninput event is specified, and when it occurs, the input text will go into the displaytext string. This is useful, because it gets displayed right away, rather than the onchange event, which requires for the input to lose focus for it to occur. This example is most common, and most other event/HTML tag combinations likely will not work.

Listing 2-8. Bind on Specific Event

```
<p><input type="text" @bind:event="oninput"
@bind="displaytext" /></p>
<p>@displaytext</p>
```

```
@code {
    string displaytext = "";
}
```

In general, the value that you bind needs to be present in the event arguments for the event specified.

Events

The code section is where the C# methods for the front end are added. The code sections are meant to contain your code for the client side, variables, and methods. It is much like a <script> tag in a standard HTML page, but there's more to it, as shown in Listing 2-9.

Listing 2-9. Variable Display

```
<p>@testvar</p>
@code {
  string testvar = "test variable";
}
```

In Listing 2-9, a variable is declared, and then it is added to a paragraph tag. This is quite special, as shown in Listing 2-10.

Listing 2-10. Onclick Event

```
<p>@testvar</p>
<p><button @onclick="@testmethod">change</button></p>
@code {
  string testvar = "test variable";
  void testmethod() {
    testvar = "test";
  }
}
```

13

In Listing 2-10, the same variable as in Listing 2-9 is declared and then displayed in the paragraph tag. There's also a C# method, which, in client-side Blazor, will run on the front end. The method is called by declaring it in the onclick event attribute for the button tag, but parentheses should not be used. The method simply changes the value for the variable, and in turn what is displayed in the paragraph tag is also changed. So, that is a oneway binding, and in Listing 2-11, a two-way binding is shown.

Listing 2-11. Bind, Onclick, and Display

```
<p>@testvar</p>
<p><input @bind="@testvar"></p>
<p><button @onclick="@(() => testmethod())">change</button></p>
@code {
   string testvar = "nothing to display";
   void testmethod()
   {
     testvar = "test value";
   }
}
```

In Listing 2-11, an input tag is bound to the testvar variable, so whenever the input tag value changes, the variable will also change, and therefore the display in the paragraph tag also changes. Do note that the input tag must lose focus for it to take effect.

So, that is how to call a method accepting no parameters. While it is not recommended, Listing 2-12 shows how to pass and accept parameters. Your method could also be a Task method, and you would be able to await it in that lambda expression.

Listing 2-12. Method with Parameters

```
<p>@testvar</p>
<p><input @bind="@testvar"></p>
<p><button @onclick="@( () => testmethod("test var"))">change
</button></p>
@code {
  string testvar = "nothing to display";
  void testmethod(string testparam)
  {
    testvar = testparam;
  }
}
```

In Listing 2-12, the method accepts the testparam parameter. So, use parentheses on the method call, and pass the value to call the method, rather than declaring it for the event almost like a variable. Use a lambda expression, and then use the method normally. This can be useful if different values are needed in the list output. To use a Task method, a lambda expression should be used as well.

As shown in Listing 2-13, it is quite easy to do, but it is recommended to use the await keyword and use a Task with an async method.

Listing 2-13. Asynchronous Task

```
<p>@testvar</p>
<p><input @bind="@testvar" /></p>
<p><button @onclick="@(async () => await
testmethod())">change</button></p>
@code {
  string testvar = "nothing to display";
  async Task testmethod()
  {
```

15

```
    testvar = "test value";
  }
}
```

Finally, you are not limited to one method; there is also an option to execute several methods in each event and/or simply set variables directly in the event.

In Listing 2-14, you can see how a Boolean variable is set to true when the button is clicked, without the use of an additional method. In that area, you could also execute additional methods or use if statements and other logic. If you want to use await, you will simply need to add the async keyword like you saw in the previous example. This option can make your code look cleaner in the code section, but it should not be abused as it might make the HTML part a lot less readable.

Listing 2-14. Direct Use of Event

```
<p><button @onclick="@(() => { buttonclicked = true; })">Click
button</button></p>
@code {
  bool buttonclicked = false;

}
```

Event Arguments

Each event has its own argument; for example, the input contains the input text. In a way, this is how bindings work; you just do not have to access the arguments directly. But there are cases where you need to, so here is how to do it.

In Listing 2-15, you can see the `oninput` event being used and the argument from that assigned to the `testvar` string. To retrieve an argument, you simply set a name in the setup for the event. This variable in this case is an object (it can be converted to a string, but for numerics you can use `double`, `int`, or something else).

Listing 2-15. Event Overrides

```
<p>@testvar</p>
<p><input @oninput="@((args) => { testvar = args.Value.
ToString(); })" /></p>
@code {
   string testvar = "";

}
```

It is important to note that the arguments for the events in Blazor and in JavaScript are not always the same.

Page and Component Lifecycle Events

Whenever the user loads a page (or a component), some events are triggered. These can be used to invoke your procedures on various stages of a page/component cycle.

The first and likely most common event is `OnInitializedAsync` (Listing 2-16). This event occurs before the page gets rendered. If you have to pull data and display it without user input, this is where such procedures should go.

Listing 2-16. Event Overrides

```
@page "/"
<h1>Index page</h1>
@code {
protected override Task OnInitializedAsync()
    {
        return base.OnInitializedAsync();
    }
 }
```

After the page gets rendered, the OnAfterRenderAsync event occurs (Listing 2-17). This can be used for procedures that require UI elements to be fully loaded.

Listing 2-17. Event Overrides

```
protected override Task OnAfterRenderAsync(bool firstRender)
    {
        return base.OnAfterRenderAsync(firstRender);
    }
```

This event will also recur if there are any updates to the page or if StateHasChanged() has been invoked (covered later in the book). Therefore, if you want to use it only on the initial render, you can check if the Boolean value is true.

Finally, OnParametersSetAsync (Listing 2-18) will occur when a new parameter is set. You will learn more about parameters later in the book; this event mostly applies to components.

Listing 2-18. Event Overrides

```
protected override Task OnParametersSetAsync()
    {
        return base.OnParametersSetAsync();
    }
```

Summary

You now know some basics of Blazor, as well as the most important parts of it: bindings and method executions. In the next chapters, we will dive deeper into Blazor and explore the differences between the different types. With that, we will not forget the basics, and you will see something from this chapter occurring in almost every example of code in this book.

CHAPTER 3

Blazor Components and Navigation

This chapter will introduce the specifics of Blazor pages and components. You will learn how page files are created and how navigation is set up. Then you will learn all that you need to know about components and their features, such as parameters, custom events, and more.

Pages and Navigation

In general, a page in Blazor is a `.razor` file that contains your code, and it has a route to it specified in the code. It can also read parameters, and that same file can act as a component, which you will learn more about later in this chapter.

Page files should be added to the `Pages` folder in your Blazor project or in subfolders of that folder. The location of the file does not matter; the page route will depend on what you specify in `@page`. Listing 3-1 demonstrates this.

In the following example, you can see two pages. The index page always has an empty route by default, as shown in Listing 3-1. The second page is called page 1, and the route specified for it is `page1`. The structure of this statement is very important. First you use the `@page` directive; then you follow that by a route enclosed in quotation marks and starting with the / character, as shown in Listing 3-2.

© Taurius Litvinavicius 2023

T. Litvinavicius, *Exploring Blazor*, https://doi.org/10.1007/978-1-4842-8768-2_3

Listing 3-1. Contents of Page1.razor

```
@page "/page1"
<p>page 1</p>
```

Listing 3-2. Contents of Index.razor

```
@page "/"
<p><a href="/page1">navigate to page 1</a></p>
```

Pages can also have parameters passed on navigation. This can be achieved in two ways; you can do it using Blazor-specific techniques, which is a more modern, easier, but also somewhat limited option. Or, you can simply parse and read the URL of the page, as shown in Listing 3-3.

Listing 3-3. Contents of Page1.razor with Parameter

```
@page "/page1/{ExampleParam}"
<p>page 1</p>
@code {
[Parameter]
Public string ExampleParam { get; set; }
}
```

For the first option, you will need to declare a variable for `Parameter` in the page file. The structure of this is important. You need to use `[Parameter]`, it has to be `public,` and it has to have `{ get; set; }`. Finally, this will work only for a string, although in components it is possible to use other types too. In addition, it has to be declared in the route string, as shown in Listing 3-4.

Listing 3-4. Contents of Index.razor

```
@page "/"
<p><a href="/page1/paramvalue">navigate to page 1</a></p>
```

You can have several parameters (Listing 3-5); however, the route that you set has to be fully complete to navigate to. In this case, any link to that page must contain those two parameters in that same exact order.

Listing 3-5. Contents of Page1.razor

```
@page "/page1/{ExampleParam1}/{ ExampleParam2}"
<p>page 1</p>
@code {
[Parameter]
public string ExampleParam1 { get; set; }
public string ExampleParam2 { get; set; }

}
```

If you want to have more flexibility, you can set several routes (Listing 3-6). This example allows navigating with both parameters, with one parameter, or without parameters at all. In such cases, the parameter properties set in the page would simply have their default values.

Listing 3-6. Contents of Page1.razor

```
@page "/page1/{ExampleParam1}/{ ExampleParam2}"
@page "/page1/{ExampleParam1}"
@page "/page1"
```

Parameters can be accessed on the life-cycle events starting from the first one, OnInitializedAsync (refer to Chapter 2).

Components

Components are the same files as pages, with pretty much the same features. But instead of being navigated to, they are declared inside pages. See Listings 3-7 and 3-8.

Listing 3-7. Contents of ExampleComponent.razor

```
<p>Example Component</p>
```

Listing 3-8. Contents of Page1.razor

```
@page "/"

<p>Index Page</p>

<ExampleComponent></ExampleComponent>
```

In this basic example, we have a new Razor file (`ExampleComponent.razor`) created in the `Pages` folder. As you can see in Figure 3-1, the component simply blends into the parent page (or component) code. And it is declared like any other HTML element.

Index Page

Example Component

Figure 3-1. *Page with component display*

If the component were placed in a different folder, you might have to declare the whole path. For example, if the component were in the `Components` folder, which is in the `Pages` folder, the statement would then be `<Pages.Components.ExampleComponent>`.

Parameters

In Listing 3-9, we have two parameters: one string and one DateTime. In components, a parameter can be whatever type you want such as your own custom object and another type.

Listing 3-9. Contents of ExampleComponent.razor

```
<p>Example Component</p>
<p>@param_string: @param_date.ToString()</p>
@code {
    [Parameter]
    public string param_string { get; set; }

    [Parameter]
    public DateTime param_date { get; set; }
}
```

The parameters are set directly in the component declaration (Listing 3-10), similar to how you would set parameters for HTML elements.

Listing 3-10. Contents of Index.razor

```
@page "/"

<p><input @bind="@forstringparam" @bind:event="oninput" /></p>

<ExampleComponent param_string="@forstringparam" param_date=
"@DateTime.UtcNow"></ExampleComponent>

@code {

    string forstringparam { get; set; }

}
```

Figure 3-2 shows the result; when the string parameter binds, it will bind on every change of the input box without having to lose focus on the input.

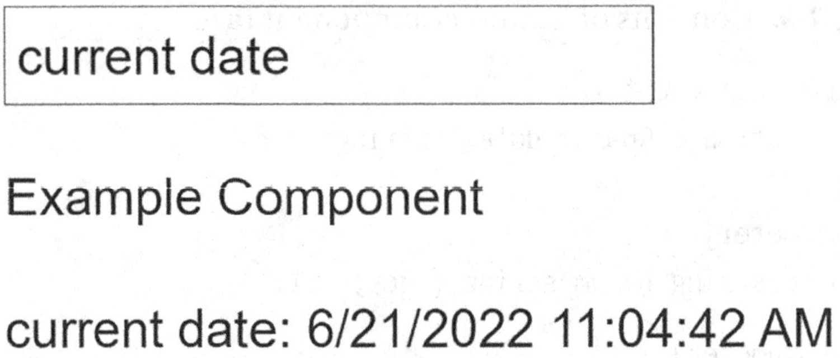

```
current date
```

Example Component

current date: 6/21/2022 11:04:42 AM

Figure 3-2. *The results yielded by Listing 3-10*

Custom Events in Components

Components can take data from a parent, but they can also return data to the parent (component or page). This can be done as a two-way binding. Also, it can have your custom events, possibly with event arguments.

In Listing 3-11, we have a basic event (with no arguments). An event is essentially a parameter of a specific type that is EventCallback. You also need to make sure to have Parameter, public, and {get; set;} in that statement for it to work.

To invoke the event, you simply use the InvokeAsync method.

Listing 3-11. Contents of ExampleComponent.razor

```
<button @onclick="@UseExampleEvent">Try it!</button>

@code {

    [Parameter]
    public EventCallback ExampleEvent {get; set;}

    async Task UseExampleEvent()
    {
```

```
    await ExampleEvent.InvokeAsync();
  }

}
```

Your custom event (Listing 3-12) is used the same as the regular HTML such as onclick and others (refer to Chapter 2).

Listing 3-12. Contents of Index.razor

```
@page "/"

<p><ExampleComponent ExampleEvent="@HandleExampleEvent">
</ExampleComponent></p>
<p>@result</p>

@code {
    string result;

    async Task HandleExampleEvent()
    {
        result = "Event has been used";
    }
}
```

If you want to provide event arguments, you just need to declare the argument type in the EventCallback setup. In this example, it is a string, but it can be anything you want. Then, the data is provided in the parameters for the InvokeAsync method (Listing 3-13).

Listing 3-13. Contents of ExampleComponent.razor

```
<button @onclick="@UseExampleEvent">Try it!</button>

@code {

    [Parameter]
    public EventCallback<string> ExampleEvent {get; set;}

    async Task UseExampleEvent()
    {
        await ExampleEvent.InvokeAsync("Event has been used");
    }

}
```

Once again, to handle the invoked event, you do it the same way as you would for regular HTML element events (Listing 3-14).

Listing 3-14. Contents of Index.razor

```
@page "/"

<p><ExampleComponent ExampleEvent="@HandleExampleEvent">
</ExampleComponent></p>
<p>@result</p>

@code {
    string result;

    async Task HandleExampleEvent(string argument)
    {
        result = argument;
    }
}
```

And just like in generic events, you can forgo the method setup (Listing 3-15).

Listing 3-15. Contents of Index.razor

```
@page "/"

<p><ExampleComponent ExampleEvent="@((argument) => { result =
argument;})"></ExampleComponent></p>
<p>@result</p>

@code {
    string result;
}
```

Custom Binds in Components

Just like you can have custom events, you can also have custom binds in your events and then use them exactly like you would in regular HTML.

To establish a binding, you will need to use a parameter property and a custom event. The EventCallback type should be the same as a parameter; it should also have the same name except the event parameter needs to end with the word Changed.

The binding will occur when InvokeAsync (Listing 3-16) is executed and the new value is passed.

Listing 3-16. Contents of ExampleComponent.razor

```
<button @onclick="@(() => { ExampleValueChanged.
InvokeAsync("test value"); })">Add value</button>
@code {

    [Parameter]
```

```
public EventCallback<string> ExampleValueChanged
{get; set;}

[Parameter]
public string ExampleValue {get; set;}
}
```

To use it, you need to specify the parameter with the bind property
(Listing 3-17).

Listing 3-17. Contents of Index.razor

```
@page "/"

<p><ExampleComponent @bind-ExampleValue="@result"
></ExampleComponent></p>
<p>@result</p>

@code {
    string result;
}
```

You can also have several events for the same bind property (Listing 3-18)
(Parameter). To do this, in the component you will have to add another
event (no rules for the name) and then invoke it where you need it.

Listing 3-18. Contents of ExampleComponent.razor

```
<button @onclick="@(() => {  SecondEvent.InvokeAsync("test
value"); })">Add value</button>
@code {

    [Parameter]
    public EventCallback<string> SecondEvent {get; set;}

    [Parameter]
```

```
public EventCallback<string> ExampleValueChanged
{get; set;}

[Parameter]
public string ExampleValue {get; set;}
}
```

Then in your page (or parent component), you will need to specify the event on which to bind (Listing 3-19). This is the same as you would do with regular HTML, for example, oninput for the input tag.

Listing 3-19. Contents of Index.razor

```
@page "/"

<p><ExampleComponent @bind-ExampleValue="@result" @bind-Example
Value:event="SecondEvent" ></ExampleComponent></p>
<p>@result</p>

@code {
    string result;
}
```

Layouts

The pages are loaded inside a layout in Blazor; this can be modified in the MainLayout.razor file, which can be found in the Shared folder.

The most important part is @body (Listing 3-20). This is where your pages will be generated. By default, you will get an example layout, but before building a real-world application, you should get rid of it all and make your custom base layout.

Listing 3-20. Contents of MainLayout.razor (Default Template)

```
<div class="page">
    <div class="sidebar">
        <NavMenu />
    </div>

    <main>
        <div class="top-row px-4">
            <a href="https://docs.microsoft.com/aspnet/"
            target="_blank">About</a>
        </div>

        <article class="content px-4">
            @Body
        </article>
    </main>
</div>
```

In the default setup, the pages will go into the article tag of HTML. The end result is that the page is displayed to the right of the navigation menu (Figure 3-3).

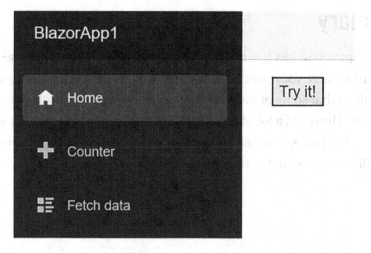

Figure 3-3. *The results yielded by the code in Listing 3-20*

Listing 3-21. Contents of MainLayout.razor

```
<div>

        @Body

</div>
```

If you remove all the default code and simply place @body in a div, the end result will look like Figure 3-4.

Figure 3-4. *The results yielded by Listing 3-21*

Summary

In this chapter, you saw lots of features for pages and components, as well as ways to arrange your code in a readable and useful way. You may also have noticed that some of the features may not seem very intuitive for regular use. However, a lot of these will be useful when building Blazor libraries, which are sets of Blazor code for others to use. That and a lot more will be covered in the upcoming chapters.

CHAPTER 4

Specifics of Different Types of Blazor

Different types of Blazor, also known as *hosting models*, are in general similar, but there are a few differences that must be remembered to avoid malfunctions in your projects. In some cases, certain things simply will not work on one of the types, or the behavior of a feature might change depending on the Blazor type.

In this chapter, you'll learn the following:

- Overview of default Visual Studio templates

- Handling API access in Blazor

Default Template Overview

You will find some interesting differences between the client-side (WebAssembly) and server-side templates. You will also learn how to customize things when needed.

Blazor Server-Side Template

For the Blazor server-side version, you have two template options at the moment. One is called "Blazor server app," which includes some example code that you will have to remove once you start your project; the other

© Taurius Litvinavicius 2023
T. Litvinavicius, *Exploring Blazor*, https://doi.org/10.1007/978-1-4842-8768-2_4

is "Blazor server app empty," which is the one you should choose for this chapter (see Figure 4-1). The Blazor server version essentially runs all its logic on your servers and sends rendered pages to be displayed in a browser. The input and output interactions are done via an active WebSocket.

Figure 4-1. *File contents of the "Blazor server app empty" template*

In the Blazor server version, you get several default files (shown in Figure 4-1), which, for the most part, should not be modified. Listing 4-1 shows the default contents of the `Program.cs` file.

Listing 4-1. Program.cs Default Contents

```
builder.Services.AddRazorPages();
builder.Services.AddServerSideBlazor();
```

In `Program.cs`, the two Blazor-related services shown in Listing 4-2 must be added; if these statements are removed, it will not work.

Listing 4-2. Program.cs Default Contents

```
app.MapBlazorHub();
app.MapFallbackToPage("/_Host");
```

After that, the Blazor navigation must be mapped; otherwise, your application will not work. However, the fallback page can be modified if you want to use another file name for _Host.cshtml. But notice that the fallback page is a Razor (.cshtml) file, not a Blazor file (.razor). Navigation in general is handled by default in App.razor, which should not be modified except for the "not found" display.

MainLayout.razor (Listing 4-3) contains a declaration of where all the pages will be rendered. The @body can be wrapped in a div or other container instead.

Listing 4-3. Default Contents of MainLayout.razor

```
@inherits LayoutComponentBase

<main> @Body </main>
```

Finally, the _Host.cshtml file is where your Blazor project is rendered. This is where you can declare your JavaScript files and your CSS styles.

Blazor Client-Side (WebAssembly) Template

The two main differences between the client- and server-side hosting models are the contents of Program.cs and the lack of a _Host.cshtml file in the client-side Blazor version (Figure 4-2).

Figure 4-2. *File contents of the "Blazor WebAssembly app empty"*
template

Now, let's take a look at the default code for Program.cs (Listing 4-4).

Listing 4-4. Default Code for Program.cs in the "Blazor
webassembly app Empty" Template

```
var builder = WebAssemblyHostBuilder.CreateDefault(args);
builder.RootComponents.Add<App>("#app");
builder.RootComponents.Add<HeadOutlet>("head::after");

builder.Services.AddScoped(sp => new HttpClient { BaseAddress =
new Uri(builder.HostEnvironment.BaseAddress) });

await builder.Build().RunAsync();
```

The Program.cs file first declares into what HTML tag everything will
be rendered and sets up the head. You may notice that this is basically
the equivalent of what the _Host.cshtml file handles in the Blazor server.
None of this should be modified, as it may cause issues or cause the
program to stop working. What you can modify is your base address if you
are using HttpClient injections to connect to your API.

To declare your JavaScript and CSS files in the client-side Blazor version, you will need to go to index.html (found in the wwwroot folder) and do it there.

Injection

Dependency injection is mainly important for the server-side Blazor projects. When injected, methods from that class can be accessed in any page or component. To understand this better, Figure 4-3 shows an example of a very basic Blazor server application (Listing 4-3).

Figure 4-3. *File contents for the example project*

In Listing 4-5, we have one service class (Calculators) that will be injected in Index.razor.

Listing 4-5. Index.razor

```
public class Calculators
    {
        public async Task<double> Calculate(double a, double b)
        {
            return a + b;
        }
    }
```

The class itself contains only one method, which adds two double values.

To inject a class, you need to use the @inject directive (Listing 4-6).

Listing 4-6. . Use of Inject in a Blazor Page

```
@page "/"
@inject Services.Calculators calculators

<p><button @onclick="(async() => { result = await calculators.
Calculate(5,5); })">Calculate</button></p>
<p>@result</p>

@code {
    double result;
}
```

However, if you ran this right now and executed the method, it would throw a major exception.

```
builder.Services.AddSingleton< Services.Calculators>();
```

To make this work, you need to declare this service in Program.cs.

Static Values

Static values must be used with caution in server-side projects. Although they can be beneficial to hold global variable data, it is important to remember that these values will be used between sessions. To demonstrate this problem, Listing 4-7 is a basic example.

Listing 4-7. StaticValues.cs Class in Blazor Server Project

```
public class StaticValues
    {
        public static string StaticValue;
    }
```
Server side Blazor project contains one class with one static string called StaticValue.
```
<p><input @bind-value="StaticValues.StaticValue" @bind-
value:event="oninput" /></p>
<p>@StaticValues.StaticValue</p>
```

In Index.razor (Listing 4-7), we have an input that binds straight to the static variable, and the value is displayed (Figure 4-4).

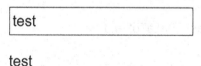

test

Figure 4-4. *Result of the example page*

If the word *test* is inserted, the result in the browser is as shown in Figure 4-4. However, if you open another browser and paste the URL for the running application, you will see the same thing without having to insert anything into the input.

41

Calling APIs

The client-side Blazor project will likely require accessing one or more APIs at some point as the logic of it runs directly on the browser. For this you can use HttpClient in a more traditional manner, or if you use JSON, you can access that directly. Listing 4-8 shows how to do it.

Listing 4-8. API Controller Example

```
public class ExampleController : Controller
    {
        [Route("testget")]
        public string TestGET()
        {
            return "test result";
        }
        [Route("testpost")]
        public string TestPOST([FromBody]DataToSend data)
        {
            return data.val1 + data.val2;
        }
        public  class DataToSend
        {
            public string val1 { get; set; }
            public bool val2 { get; set; }
        }
    }
```

For the example controller, we have two basic routes: one for the GET and one for the POST Listing 4-9. You may also notice the data model class; an exact match will have to be provided in the Blazor project as well. Alternatively, if you have more of these model classes, you may use a class library to store them.

Listing 4-9. HttpClient in the Blazor Page

```
@page "/"
@inject HttpClient http
<p><button @onclick="@RequestData" >Request data</button></p>
<p>Result: @result</p>
<p><button @onclick="@SendData" >Send data</button></p>

@code {

    string result;

    DataToSend datatosend = new DataToSend();

    async Task RequestData()
    {
        result = await http.GetFromJsonAsync<string>
        ("testget");
    }

    async Task SendData()
    {
        datatosend.val2 = true;
        result = await (await http.
        PostAsJsonAsync<DataToSend>("/testget",datatosend)).
        Content.ReadFromJsonAsync<string>();
    }

    class DataToSend
    {
        public string val1 { get; set; }
        public bool val2 { get; set; }
    }
}
```

To access the JSON-based API, you use either one of two methods: PostAsJsonAsync or GetFromJsonAsync. For PostAsJsonAsync, you will need to supply the class object that you are sending, and the API must have a class in the same structure to be able to receive the data. The response of that is an HTTP response, which contains content and a few other things. To read JSON content, you will need to use ReadFromJsonAsync, which gives you the same result as FetFromJsonAsync.

Adding the API Controller

The server-side Blazor project runs in a similar way to the .NET web API, which means that you can integrate this capability into your Blazor project.

This will require adding a Controllers folder (and controller classes) and a few things in Program.cs. A good quick way to do it is to simply create an empty API project and copy things that apply to API handling from there. As you can see in Figure 4-5, a Controllers folder has been added and, inside it, a new controller file Listing 4-10.

Figure 4-5. Example project files

Listing 4-10. Method Execution from Program.cs

```
app.MapControllers();
```

For this to work, you need to add `MapControllers` in the `Program.cs` file.

```
public class ExampleController : Controller
    {
        [Route("/testroute")]
        public async Task<string> TestRoute()
        {
            return "test";
        }

    }
```

The controller itself will look and work the same as it would in a regular .NET API project.

Blazor Hosted

When creating a new Blazor project in Visual Studio, you get a few options, and one of them is Blazor hosted. This type simply adds an API project to a sort of shared assembly with your Blazor client project, as shown in Figure 4-6.

Figure 4-6. *Projects contained in a Blazor hosted assembly*

The Client one is your Blazor client project, the Server one is your API project to which you can add controllers, and finally Shared is a class library that can host shared logic and/or data models. You will later see a basic example done with this and other types of Blazor.

Basic Form Example for Two Types of Blazor

This will be a basic example of a user registration form (Figure 4-7) in the three Blazor types: server, client, and with hosted arrangements.

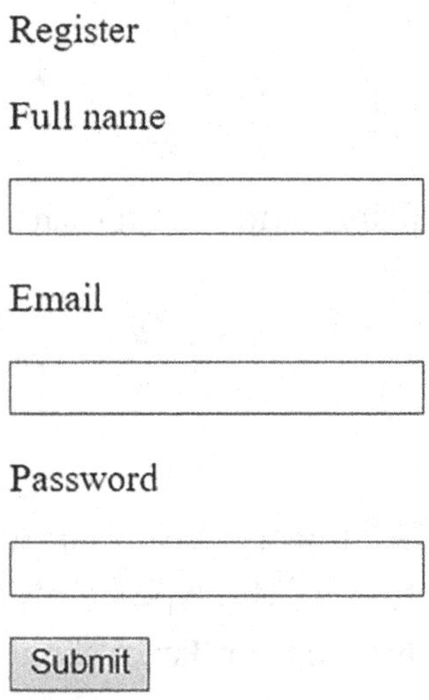

Register

Full name

Email

Password

Submit

Figure 4-7. *Basic form example view*

You will see the differences between the types and read explanations on why one is better or worse than the other.

We'll now look at the Blazor server version with a simple one-project arrangement (Figure 4-8).

Figure 4-8. *Blazor server project files*

The form itself will go into the default Index.razor file, and the logic will go in UserData.cs (Listing 4-11).

Listing 4-11. UserData class contents

```
public class UserData
    {
        public async Task<bool> InsertNewUser(User newuser)
        {
            //insert into DB
            return true;
        }

        public class User
        {
            public string FullName { get; set; }
            public string Email { get; set; }
            public string Password { get; set; }
        }
    }
```

The service class simply contains the method, which when executed would insert the data into the database. There is also a data model class for the form data.

The interface part (Listing 4-12) uses the data model and binds the inputs. Then on the click of the button, it executes the method to insert data into the database. The UI itself will be the same as in the other Blazor types.

Listing 4-12. UserData.cs

```
@page "/"
@inject Services.UserData userdata

<p>Register</p>

<p>Full name</p>
<p><input @bind="NewUser.FullName" /></p>

<p>Email</p>
<p><input @bind="NewUser.Email" /></p>

<p>Password</p>
<p><input @bind="NewUser.Password" /></p>

<p><button @onclick="@Submit" >Submit</button></p>

@code {
    Services.UserData.User NewUser = new Services.
UserData.User();

    async Task Submit(){
     bool result =  await  userdata.InsertNewUser(NewUser);
    }
}
```

For the client-side part, you will also need an API project, which contains one controller (Listing 4-13) with a class model for data.

Listing 4-13. UsersController.cs

```
public class UsersController : Controller
    {
        [Route("adduser")]
        public async Task<bool> AddUser([FromBody]User user)
        {
            // insert into DB
        }

        public class User
        {
            public string FullName { get; set; }
            public string Email { get; set; }
            public string Password { get; set; }
        }
    }
```

Listing 4-14. Index.razor

```
@page "/"
@inject HttpClient http

<p>Register</p>

<p>Full name</p>
<p><input @bind="NewUser.FullName" /></p>

<p>Email</p>
<p><input @bind="NewUser.Email" /></p>

<p>Password</p>
```

```
<p><input @bind="NewUser.Password" /></p>

<p><button @onclick="@Submit">Submit</button></p>

@code {

    User NewUser = new  User();

    async Task Submit()
    {
        bool result = await  (await http.
PostAsJsonAsync<User>("/adduser",NewUser)).Content.
ReadFromJsonAsync<bool>();
    }

    public class User
    {
        public string FullName { get; set; }
        public string Email { get; set; }
        public string Password { get; set; }
    }
}
```

Instead of injecting and executing a method like you would in the server-side version, here you need to make an API call (Listing 4-14). You will also need to set up the base address for HttpClient in Program.cs.

The Blazor hosted option is basically the same as on the client side. We have a client-side Blazor and .NET API, but in this case we also have a class library project (Figure 4-9).

Figure 4-9. *Projects and project files*

The difference in the controller is only that the data model comes from a class library (Listing 4-15).

Listing 4-15. UsersController.cs

```
public class UsersController : Controller
    {
        [Route("adduser")]
        public async Task AddUser([FromBody] Shared.User user)
        {
            // insert into DB
        }
    }
```

However, you can achieve a similar result without having this hosted arrangement. You can simply have a class library that you use on both projects: client-side Blazor and .NET API.

The Blazor server part (Listing 4-16) is pretty much the same as in client Blazor, except that the data model class is in a library. The difference from the server-side version is that we make an API call instead of executing a method directly.

Listing 4-16. Index.razor

```
@page "/"
@inject HttpClient http

<p>Register</p>

<p>Full name</p>
<p><input @bind="NewUser.FullName" /></p>

<p>Email</p>
<p><input @bind="NewUser.Email" /></p>

<p>Password</p>
<p><input @bind="NewUser.Password" /></p>

<p><button @onclick="@Submit">Submit</button></p>

@code {

    Shared.User NewUser = new  Shared.User();

    async Task Submit()
    {
        bool result = await  (await http.PostAsJsonAsync<Shared.
User>("/adduser",NewUser)).Content.ReadFromJsonAsync<bool>();
    }

}
```

Multiple Select Example

This example shows how a multiple select can be made using only basic buttons and C# code in Blazor. The system is quite simple; we have four select options, and whichever option is selected is highlighted in blue with the number displayed on top (Figure 4-10).

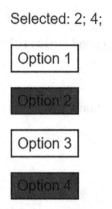

Figure 4-10. *Custom-made multiselect*

For the values (Listing 4-17), we have a basic dictionary, which contains the number of the selection, and a Boolean value, which determines if it is selected or not. In addition, we also have a method that simply outputs a string for the background color statement in CSS. For a more complicated styling change, you could use CSS classes instead.

Listing 4-17. Code Part of the Blazor File

```
@code  {

    Dictionary<int, bool> Selections = new
Dictionary<int, bool>()
        {
            { 1, true},
            { 2, false},
```

```
                { 3, false},
                { 4, false}
        };

    string GenerateColorForSelection(bool is_selected)
    {
        if (is_selected)
        {
            return "background-color:blue;";
        }else
        {
            return "background-color:white;";
        }

    }
}
```

In the HTML part (see Listing 4-18), we have four buttons representing four selections. When a button is clicked, the Boolean value for that specific selection changes. Then the method to generate the background color is used to set the color according to the selection status. Then, the foreach loop goes through the dictionary and displays the values that are selected.

Listing 4-18. UI Part of the Blazor File

```
<p>Selected:

    @foreach (var item in Selections.Where(opt =>
    opt.Value == true))
    {
        @(item.Key + "; ")
    }
    </p>
```

```
<p><button style="@GenerateColorForSelection(Selections[1])"
@onclick="@(() => { Selections[1] = Selections[1] == false ?
true :  false;  })">Option 1</button></p>
<p><button style="@GenerateColorForSelection(Selections[2])"
@onclick="@(() => { Selections[2] = Selections[2] == false ?
true :  false;  })">Option 2</button></p>
<p><button style="@GenerateColorForSelection(Selections[3])"
@onclick="@(() => { Selections[3] = Selections[3] == false ?
true :  false;  })">Option 3</button></p>
<p><button style="@GenerateColorForSelection(Selections[4])"
@onclick="@(() => { Selections[4] = Selections[4] == false ?
true :  false;  })">Option 4</button></p>
```

You can reuse this, but it must be in a component, and you must use parameters with custom events (see Chapter 3). This will also work on any of the Blazor types.

Summary

In this chapter you saw useful features for different Blazor types and the differences between them. But in the end, the choice of Blazor type will always depend on your specific use case. In the following chapter, you will learn about several useful features that can be applied to all Blazor types: accessing JavaScript, using local storage, and more.

CHAPTER 5

General Blazor

In this chapter, you will find all the important features of Blazor that were not covered in previous chapters as well as some use case examples to go with them. Specifically, you'll learn about the following:

- JavaScript interactions

- Local storage with Blazor

- Handling files

- Background tasks and examples

Interact with JavaScript

Although Blazor runs fully on C#, you will sometimes find cases where you will be required to interact with JavaScript, such as when executing JavaScript functions from C# or executing C# methods from JavaScript. Or you might want to use third-party JavaScript libraries and access browser features that are not available directly via Blazor.

The project we'll use to demonstrate this is a server-side project; it simply contains the original `Index.razor` file and the newly added `ExampleJS.js` file (as shown in Figure 5-1).

© Taurius Litvinavicius 2023
T. Litvinavicius, *Exploring Blazor*, https://doi.org/10.1007/978-1-4842-8768-2_5

Figure 5-1. *File contents of the example project*

For now the JavaScript simply contains one function (Listing 5-1), which will take a string value from C# and set it in JavaScript. Later we'll add more code to see how JavaScript can execute C# methods.

Listing 5-1. JavaScript Code

```
var JSvalue;

function SetValue(newvalue) {
    Jsvalue = newvalue;
}
```

To execute the JavaScript function from C# (Listing 5-2), you will need to add the IJSRuntime injection. Then use InvokeVoidAsync and set the name of the function followed by any arguments the function takes. If the function returns a value, you will need to use the InvokeAsync method and declare the type of the returned value.

Listing 5-2. Blazor Code

```
@page "/"
@inject IJSRuntime js

<p><button @onclick="SetValueInJS" >Set value in JS
</button></p>

@code {

    async Task SetValueInJS()
    {
        await js.InvokeVoidAsync("SetValue", "testvalue");
    }

}
```

For the second part, we add two more functions (Listing 5-3): one that will be executed on the click of a button and then execute the C# method and another that sets the reference for the page (or it could be a component). The C# method is executed by using the function InvokeMethodAsync, which takes the name of the method followed by any parameters it takes.

Listing 5-3. JavaScript Code

```
var JSvalue;

var pageref;

function SetValue(newvalue) {
    JSvalue = newvalue;
}

function RetrieveValue() {
```

```
    pageref.invokeMethodAsync('RetrieveJSValue', JSvalue);
}

function SetPageReference(pagereference) {
    pageref = pagereference;
}
```

The UI part (Listing 5-4) has been expanded further too. It now contains the page reference variable (DotNetObjectReference). For this to work, you will need to create the page reference in the setup (before using it); in this case, it is done on the OnInitializedAsync method, and the function is JavaScript, which is used to set the reference there.

Listing 5-4. Blazor Code

```
@page "/"
@inject IJSRuntime js

<p><button @onclick="SetValueInJS" >Set value in JS
</button></p>
<p><button onclick="RetrieveValue();">Retrieve value from JS
</button></p>
<p>@jsvalue</p>

@code {
    string jsvalue;

    private DotNetObjectReference<Index> PageRef;

    protected override async Task OnInitializedAsync()
    {
        PageRef = DotNetObjectReference.Create(this);
        await js.InvokeAsync<string>("SetPageReference",
        PageRef);
    }
```

```
async Task SetValueInJS()
{
    await js.InvokeVoidAsync("SetValue", "testvalue");
}

[JSInvokableAttribute("RetrieveJSValue")]
public async Task RetrieveJSValue(string newvalue)
{
    jsvalue = newvalue;
    StateHasChanged();
}
}
```

The method that is executed from JavaScript must be public and have the JSInvokableAttribute attribute set. The parameter for that is used in the JavaScript part to find and execute that method. In this case, the method takes a value and sets it to a variable on the page. This requires StateHasChanged to be executed; otherwise, the UI will not be updated.

Code-Behind Files

Code-behind files can store CSS data and C# logic and are accessible only to that specific file (page or component). This can be useful to keep the code clean and store component-specific CSS styles more easily.

To create a CSS code-behind file, you only need to create a CSS file where your component (or page) is. The file must be named in a specific way (as shown in the example for Component1.razor shown in Figure 5-2 and Listing 5-5).

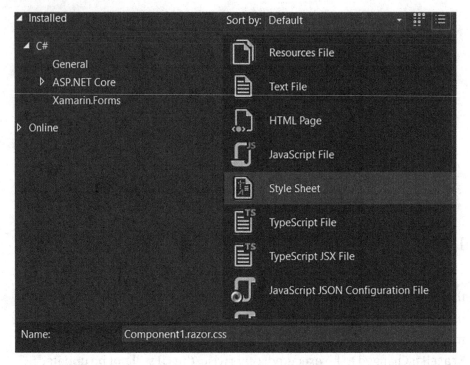

Figure 5-2. *Stylesheet file creation in Visual Studio*

Listing 5-5. YourComponentName].razor.css

```
<link href="codebehindfiles.styles.css" rel="stylesheet">
```

To make this work, you will also need to add a specific stylesheet Listing 5-6 reference in your _Host.cshtml or index.html file (on the client side). For this, you can use the following format:

```
[YourProjectName].styles.css
```

Listing 5-6. CSS Code for Example

```
.buttonclass {
    width:100px;
    background-color:blue;
    color: white;
}
```

The example in Listing 5-7 shows a basic style for button.

Listing 5-7. Buttons with CSS Classes

```
<p><button class="buttonclass" @onclick="@SetText" >Add text
</button></p>
<p class="buttonclass">@texttodisplay</p>
```

The example component contains a button to which the style is applied, and remember, the style can be applied only to elements of this component, as shown in Listing 5-7.

If you try running this example (Listing 5-8), you will see that only the button in the component has the style applied.

Listing 5-8. Index.razor Page with Example Component

```
@page "/"
<p><button class="buttonclass">Index button</button></p>
<Component1></Component1>
```

Creating a code-behind C# file is similar, but it will require some additional work. First, you need to create a C# file (.cs) based on the format shown in Figure 5-3.

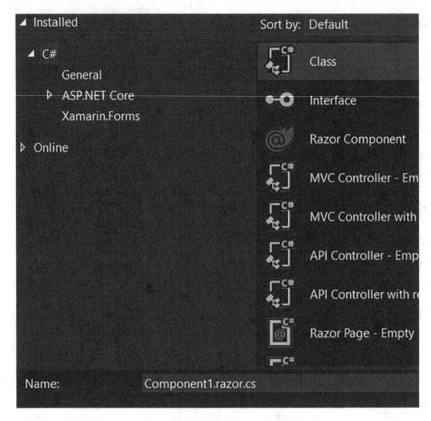

Figure 5-3. *CSS file creation in Visual Studio*

Here is the format:

[YourComponentName].razor.cs

The file is shown in Listing 5-9.

Listing 5-9. [YourComponentName].razor.cs

```
public class Component1Logic : ComponentBase
    {
        public string texttodisplay;

        public async Task SetText()
```

```
    {
        texttodisplay = "test";
    }
}
```

In the file, you will need to change the class name (without renaming the file itself) and then add inheritance for the Component base. The example simply has one method that sets the value to a string, which is displayed in the previously shown UI code (Component1.razor).

Finally, in the component itself you need to declare inheritance (Listing 5-10) for the previously created class. If you miss this step, it will not work.

Listing 5-10. Inheritance for C# Code-Behind

```
@inherits Component1Logic
```

Local Storage

Local storage in browsers can be used to store user-specific data that is carried between sessions. Blazor offers a couple of ways to access local storage, and both have their own upsides and downsides.

The first way is to use ProtectedLocalStorage (Listing 5-11), which is available only for the Blazor server version.

Listing 5-11. ProtectedLocalStorage Example

```
@using Microsoft.AspNetCore.Components.Server.
ProtectedBrowserStorage
@inject ProtectedLocalStorage  storage
```

You will first need to do an injection for ProtectedLocalStorage, and for that you will need the using statement shown in the example Listing 5-12.

Listing 5-12. Example UI Code

```
<p><input @bind="examplevalue" /></p>
<p><button @onclick="@(async () => { await  storage.SetAsync
("ExampleValue",examplevalue); })" >Set</button></p>
<p><button @onclick="@(async () => { examplevalue =
(await  storage.GetAsync<string>("ExampleValue")).Value; })"
>Get</button></p>
<p>@examplevalue</p>

@code {
    string examplevalue;
}
```

The example (Listing 5-12) here is quite straightforward; it will insert a value, and once you reload the page, you will be able to fetch that value. To add to new value, you will use SetAsync. This takes the key of the value and value itself, a basic key-value pair. Then to retrieve the value, use GetAsync and provide a matching key for your value. This feature allows you to add any type you want: numbers, strings, or your own custom objects.

If you look at the developer tools and check the local storage (Figure 5-4), you will notice that the value is encrypted. This is something to remember if you later want to access your value without using the ProtectedStorage option.

Figure 5-4. *View of developer tools in browser*

If you are working with the Blazor client-side version (WebAssembly), you will have to interact with JavaScript and connect to the LocalStorage feature directly Listing 5-13.

Listing 5-13. JavaScript Injection Example

```
@inject IJSRuntime js
```

For this you will first need to inject IJSRuntime.

```
<p><input @bind="examplevalue" /></p>
<p><button @onclick="@(async () => { await  js.
InvokeVoidAsync("localStorage.setItem","ExampleValue",example
value); })" >Set</button></p>
<p><button @onclick="@(async () => { examplevalue = await js.
InvokeAsync<string>("localStorage.getItem","ExampleValue"); })"
>Get</button></p>
<p>@examplevalue</p>

@code {
    string examplevalue;
}
```

To access local storage, you do not need to write additional JavaScript. To add a new key-value pair, you can simply access the setItem function, as shown in Listing 5-13. This will take the key as the first parameter and your value as the second.

To retrieve your item, you can use getItem, which will only require you to pass the key of the key-value pair. You will also need to declare the type of the value you retrieve. However, this will work only for basic types like double, string, and others. If you need to store something more complex, you can turn it into JSON and deserialize it after retrieving the JSON string.

Pick and Save Files

Blazor provides a way to directly pick files without having to interact with JavaScript, but for downloading (saving a file) Listing 5-14 that will not be the case.

Listing 5-14. Blazor Code for File Picker

```
<p>
    <button onclick="document.getElementById('flpicker').
click()">Pick</button>
    <InputFile id="flpicker" OnChange="@(async (args) => await
OnInputFileChange(args))" hidden multiple ></InputFile>
    <p>@filesize</p>
    <p>@filename</p>
</p>
```

To pick a file, you will need to use the default Blazor component InputFile. Styling it can be tricky; therefore, you always want to hide it and use a button for invoking the file picker instead. To do that, you will need to give the InputFile and ID and then in the button use simple JavaScript to invoke the click event Listing 5-15. Notice that we are not using Blazor to interact with JavaScript; it is done directly in the button and by using onclick rather than Blazor's @onclick. With that, you will also want to add a hidden *attribute* (to hide the InputFile) and *multiple* (if you allow users to pick multiple files).

Listing 5-15. File Picker Initialization Example

```
@code {
    long filesize;
    string filename;

    private async Task OnInputFileChange(InputFileChange
    EventArgs e)
```

```
{
    foreach (var File in e.GetMultipleFiles(e.FileCount))
    {
        filesize = File.Size;
        filename = File.Name;

        Stream str = File.OpenReadStream(1000000,
        CancellationToken.None);
    }
  }
}
```

If you have multiple files picked, you can use GetMultipleFiles to retrieve references to them. This will also work for a single file. For each file you will get some data name, size, and more. To read the file and use it, you will need to use OpenReadStream and make sure to set your custom maximum file size as the default is only around 500KB.

To download a file, several options exist, although it will have to be a custom solution. This particular example Listing 5-16 will show you one of the ways to deal with it for the Blazor client-side version.

Listing 5-16. JavaScript Code for Downloading a File in the Browser

```
function downloadfile(name, bt64) {
        var downloadlink = document.createElement('a');
        downloadlink.download = name;
        downloadlink.href = "data:application/octet-
        stream;base64," + bt64;
        document.body.appendChild(downloadlink);
        downloadlink.click();
        document.body.removeChild(downloadlink);
    }
```

For this technique, you will first need to set up a JavaScript function. This takes your desired file name and a base64 string representing your file. Then, the function creates an element (not visible anywhere), adds href for the file download, and clicks it, which initiates the download Listing 5-17.

Listing 5-17. C#/Blazor Code for Downloading the File in a Browser

```
@page "/"
@inject IJSRuntime js

<p><button @onclick="@Download">Download</button></p>

@code{
    async Task Download()
    {
        string json = System.Text.Json.JsonSerializer.
        Serialize(data);
        string base64 = Convert.ToBase64String(System.Text.
        Encoding.UTF8.GetBytes(json));
        await js.InvokeAsync<object>("downloadfile",
        "examplefile_" + DateTime.UtcNow.ToFileTimeUtc().
        ToString() + ".json",base64);

    }

    ExampleData data = new ExampleData()
        {
            val1 = "value 1",
            val2 = "value 2"
        };
```

```
class ExampleData
{
    public string val1 { get; set; }
    public string val2 { get; set; }
}

}
```

Since this is a JSON file, we first generate a JSON string from a C# object. Then we need to create a base64 string, which can be created from any object in C#, so this does not have to be JSON file. Finally, for downloading, we need to initiate the JavaScript function, and it will create a download.

Creating a Blazor Code Library

Just like any C# executable project, Blazor can have class libraries. These libraries are capable of storing not just classes with logic but also components and styling. The Blazor library project template is called Razor Class Library (Figure 5-5) in Visual Studio.

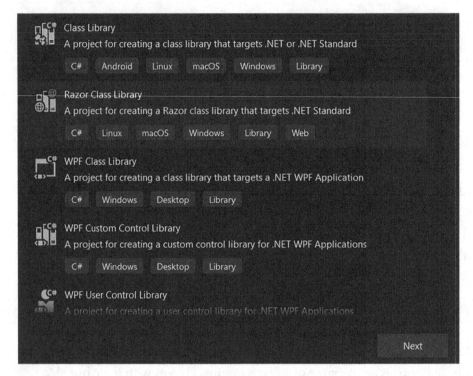

Figure 5-5. *Razor class project setup in Visual Studio*

For a basic example, we have one Blazor project and one Blazor code library project (Figure 5-6). The library contains a new CSS file and a component, which will be displayed in `Index.razor`.

Figure 5-6. *File contents for example projects*

There is only one style here (Listing 5-18) to make a button red Listing 5-19.

Listing 5-18. CSS Code

```css
.RedButton {
    background-color: red;
    color:white;
}
```

Listing 5-19. Button with CSS Class Applied

```html
<p><button class="RedButton">Example component button
</button></p>
```

The example Listing 5-20 component simply contains a button to which the style is applied.

Listing 5-20. Example Component Implementation

```
<p><button class="RedButton">Index page button</button></p>
<BlazorLibrary.ExampleComponent></BlazorLibrary.
ExampleComponent>
```

`Index.razor` contains another button, with the same style applied (from the library).

The result of the code is quite simple (Figure 5-7): two buttons are displayed. One is from the page itself, and one is from the component that comes from the library.

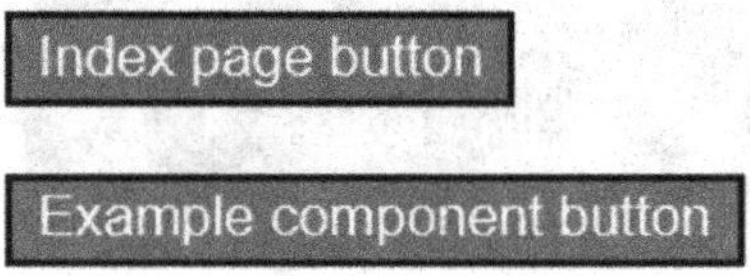

Figure 5-7. *Output view for the example*

There are two important things to do for this to work. The first is to add a reference Listing 5-21 to the library in your Blazor project, just like you would add any other code library to a C# project.

Listing 5-21. Reference for CSS File

```
    <link href="_content/BlazorLibrary/ExampleStyles.css"
rel="stylesheet" />
```

The second thing is to add the reference to the stylesheet file in a very specific way. This will apply to any JavaScript stored in the library. You must always use the following format:

```
"_content/{NameOfYourLibrary}/{LocationOrFileInWWWRoot}"
```

Background Tasks

Background tasks in Blazor need to be handled with care Listing 5-22, as any issues related to UI updates can be difficult solve.

Listing 5-22. UI Update from Background Task Example

```
<p>@fordisplay</p>

@code {
    int fordisplay;

    protected override Task OnInitializedAsync()
    {
        _ = BackgroundTask();
        return base.OnInitializedAsync();
    }

    async Task BackgroundTask()
    {
        var rnd = new Random();
        while (true)
        {
            await Task.Delay(2000);

            fordisplay = rnd.Next(1, 1000);
            StateHasChanged();
        }
    }
}
```

The example here simply runs a loop and every two seconds (2000ms) sets a new random value. The method BackgroundTask is started in OnInitializedAsync, without await, meaning that it will start running and will move to something else. This also means it will be running in a background.

For this to update the UI, you must use the StateHasChanged method. This should be used whenever a value in the UI needs to be updated.

Countdown Timer Example

This example will show several features from this and previous chapters joined together in one project.

First, in the code section, we need two variables (Listing 5-23). TimeSpan will be holding the time, and the system will be subtracting from it every second. The Status integer is simply the status for the timer. It is important to note that if you have a bigger project where such statuses would be reused, it might be worth your time to have an enum set up.

Listing 5-23. Variables for Timer

```
TimeSpan timeleft;

    // 1- running, 2 - paused, 3 - stopped
    int status = 3;
```

For the running state (Listing 5-24), we simply have a button, which when clicked will change the status variable, which in turn will change what the user sees. You will later see how the pausing of a timer is done. Once the timer is paused, the user can see a resume button, which, again, simply changes the value in the status variable.

Listing 5-24. Timer Setup and Display UI

```
@if (status == 1 || status == 2)
{
    @if (status == 1)
    {
        <p><button @onclick="@(() => { status = 2; })">Pause
        </button></p>
    }
    @if (status == 2)
    {
        <p><button @onclick="@(() => { status = 1; })">Resume
        </button></p>
    }
    <p><button @onclick="@(() => { status = 3; timeleft = new
    TimeSpan(0, 0, 0); })">Stop</button></p>

    <p>Time left: @timeleft</p>
}
```

Both paused and running views allow users to see the timer display (time left) and a stop button. When the stop button is clicked, the status variable is changed, and with that the TimeSpan variable is reset to zero.

The stopped status view (Listing 5-25) is where the user can start the countdown and set the time in seconds.

Listing 5-25. Timer Setup UI

```
@if (status == 3)
{
    <p>Seconds: <input value="@timeleft.Seconds" type="number"
@oninput="@((args) => { timeleft = new TimeSpan(0,0,Convert.
ToInt32(args.Value)); })" /></p>
```

```
<p><button @onclick="@( async () => { status = 1;
RunTimer(); })">Start</button></p>
}
```

Since we have TimeSpan for storing time, we cannot directly bind it to the input. Instead, we need to use the oninput event and get the seconds from that event argument. To complete the two-way binding, we just need to assign value that we set in the event.

Finally, the start button will change its status to running and execute the RunTimer method (Listing 5-26) without await; it will run in the background.

Listing 5-26. Method for Updating the Timer Every Second

```
async Task RunTimer()
    {
        while (status == 1 || status == 2)
        {
            await Task.Delay(1000);
            if (status == 1)
            {
                timeleft = timeleft.Subtract(new TimeSpan(0, 0, 1));
                StateHasChanged();
                if (timeleft == new TimeSpan(0, 0, 0))
                {

                    status = 3;
                    StateHasChanged();
                    break;
                }
            }
        }
    }
```

The method used in Listing 5-26 contains a loop that will run as long as the status is either running or paused. But, it will only update the value and display it in the UI if the status is running. Every second it will subtract one second from the TimeSpan variable and execute the StateHasChanged event to update the UI. Finally, once the TimeSpan reaches zero, it will change the status to stopped (3) and once again execute StateHasChanged to update the UI.

Error Boundaries

Error boundaries in Blazor can wrap specific parts of UI code, which then in case of an error would only display an error and break that part of the code. This can be useful when dealing with interactive lists and other such more complex arrangements.

In Listing 5-27, we have a class object that is set to null. Then in the paragraph it is set to display val1, which will throw an exception as the object is null. Normally, this would break the whole page, but since it is wrapped in ErrorBoundary, it will display an error only for that part of code. If you only wrap your code in ErrorBoundary, it will display the default warning. To add your own, you use ErrorContent and then add wrapped content in ChildContent.

Listing 5-27. ErrorBoundary in Blazor Code

```
<ErrorBoundary>
    <ChildContent>
        <p>@exampleclass.val1</p>
    </ChildContent>

<ErrorContent>
        <p  >Something went wrong</p>
    </ErrorContent>
```

```
</ErrorBoundary>

<p>Still works</p>

@code {
    ExampleClass exampleclass;

    class ExampleClass
    {
        public string val1 { get; set; }
    }
}
```

Summary

In this chapter, you saw lots of features of Blazor and learned that some things are possible in only one of the Blazor types. Therefore, you should always be careful when you are planning your applications and choosing Blazor types.

CHAPTER 6

Practice Tasks for Server-Side Blazor

Now that you are done with learning, you need to practice. We will start with two tasks for server-side Blazor and explore its use case further.

In this chapter, you will be able to practice the following:

- Setting up a Blazor server project

- Using UI bindings for Blazor

- Executing methods in Blazor

- Handling dependency injections in the Blazor server

Task 1

The first task will be a simple project that merely takes the data from the user interface, inserts it into a database, and then retrieves and displays the data. The server-side version is really useful in this case when you work with simple forms and you need quick access to the server.

Description

Create a product management dashboard.

© Taurius Litvinavicius 2023
T. Litvinavicius, *Exploring Blazor*, https://doi.org/10.1007/978-1-4842-8768-2_6

The user should be able to do the following:

- Insert a product

- Retrieve product list

- Delete a product

This is the product data:

- ID

- Title

- Seller's name

- Description

- Value

The product list items should also contain a button or other element, which when clicked will delete the element.

For this project, you will not need to interact with a real database; instead, a static list will be used. You can find it in the resources.

Resources

Since we are not learning about databases here, we need to create a fake one. This way, you can focus on Blazor-related matters only.

Create a `.cs` file according to the code provided (Listing 6-1). This will be your database, where you will insert your product objects, retrieve them, and delete them.

Listing 6-1. Fake Database

```
using System.Collections.Generic;
namespace BlazorApp1
{
    public class FakeDatabase
    {
      public static  List<your product model> products = new
      List<DataModels.ProductModel>();
    }
}
```

You can start this project with the nonempty Blazor server-side template.

Solution

As usual, there are many solutions to this task, but we will still take a look at one possibility and explore it as much as possible. We will start with the general setup of the project and then move to services and then to pages.

As you can see (Figure 6-1), the project (Blazor server app) has most of the default contents removed, but we still leave Index.razor, MainLayout.razor, and NavMenu.razor.

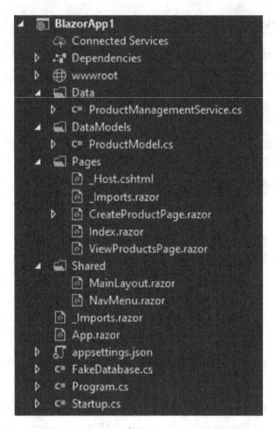

Figure 6-1. *The solution project*

First, the Shared folder (Figure 6-1) contains our main layout, as well as the nav menu where we will have the navigation options to our two pages. We also have the index page, which will contain our navigation links. In addition, we will created a couple of pages for creating new products and retrieving the list. For the logic part, we have the Data and DataModels folders. In DataModels, we will have the model for the product, and Data will contain our logic. This is a good way to lay out your project so you know exactly where to put files.

Listing 6-2 shows the contents of the ProductModel.cs file in the DataModels folder.

Listing 6-2. Product Model

```
using System;
namespace BlazorApp1.DataModels
{
    public class ProductModel
    {
        public Guid id { get;  set; }
        public string title { get; set; }
        public string sellername { get; set; }
        public string description { get; set; }
        public decimal value { get; set; }
    }
}
```

First, we need to establish the data model for the product. As you can see, it simply contains all the required properties, including an ID of type Guid. This ID needs to be referred to in your FakeDatabase class (see Listing 6-3).

Listing 6-3. Product Management Service

```
using System;
using System.Collections.Generic;
using System.Linq;
using System.Threading.Tasks;
namespace BlazorApp1.Data
{
    public class ProductManagementService
    {
        public Task<bool> CreateProductAsync(DataModels.
        ProductModel pmodel)
        {
```

```
        try
        {
            FakeDatabase.products.Add(pmodel);
            return Task.FromResult(true);
        }
        catch (Exception)
        {
            return Task.FromResult(false);
        }
    }
    public Task<List<DataModels.ProductModel>>
    GetAllProductsAsync()
    {
        return Task.FromResult(FakeDatabase.products);
    }
    public Task<bool> DeleteProductAsync(Guid id)
    {
        try
        {

            FakeDatabase.products.Remove(FakeDatabase.
            products.Where(x => x.id == id).ToArray()[0]);
            return Task.FromResult(true);
        }
        catch (Exception)
        {
            return Task.FromResult(false);
        }
    }
    }
}
```

Once we have that set up, we can move on to the logic. We will be using only one service, kind of like you would have a controller in the API. Except in this case, we have methods instead of the HTTP method parameters: POST (CreateProductAsync), GET (GetAllProductsAsync), and DELETE (DeleteProductAsync). This way, everything is conveniently placed, and it is easy to find. The first method will simply take our model object as a parameter and insert it in the list in FakeDatabase. The second one is even more basic as it returns only the list. Finally, the last one is a bit more complex; to make it more realistic, we want to pass only the ID. The Remove method in the list type takes the whole object, so in this case, we have to use a little LINQ to find it by ID.

You also have to register (Listing 6-4) your service in the Startup. cs file. Afterward, you can move on to other tasks, although it is recommended to register the service after you have created the code file.

Listing 6-4. Service Registry

```
public void ConfigureServices(IServiceCollection services)
    {
        services.AddRazorPages();
        services.AddServerSideBlazor();
        services.AddSingleton<ProductManagementService>();
    }
```

For the create page (see Listing 6-5), we can try to simplify it as much as possible by binding the variables from a constructed object rather than declaring them separately in the page. But before anything else, we establish a route for the page and inject the product management service. In the code section, we have a result string, which will simply tell us if the product was inserted successfully. After that, we declare a product variable, which has its contents bound to corresponding input fields. InsertNewProduct gets executed on the click of the button, and it executes CreateProductAsync and then checks the return Boolean. Finally, the method re-assigns the producttoinsert variable so that the new product could be inserted.

Listing 6-5. Create Product Page

```
@page "/createproductpage"
@inject Data.ProductManagementService productmanagement
<p>title</p>
<p><input @bind="@producttoinsert.title"></p>
<p>seller name</p>
<p><input @bind="@producttoinsert.sellername"></p>
<p>description</p>
<p><textarea @bind="@producttoinsert.description"></p>
<p>value</p>
<p><input @bind="@producttoinsert.value"></p>
<p><button @onclick="@(async () => await
InsertNewProduct())">Insert a product</button></p>
<p>@result</p>
@code {
        string result;
        DataModels.ProductModel producttoinsert = new
DataModels.ProductModel() { id = Guid.NewGuid() };
    async Task InsertNewProduct()
    {
        if (await productmanagement.CreateProductAsync
        (producttoinsert))
        {
            result = "product created";
            producttoinsert = new DataModels.ProductModel();
        }
        else
        {
            result = "failed to create";
        }
    }
}
```

For the product display, we have a rather complex page (see Listing 6-6), but to simplify it, we will be using a table to display our products. The alternative to that would be using components for each item.

Listing 6-6. View Products Page

```
@page "/viewproductspage"
@inject Data.ProductManagementService productmanagement
<table>
    <tbody>
        @if (products != null)
        {
            @foreach (var item in products)
            {
        <tr>
            <td>@item.id</td>
            <td>@item.title</td>
            <td>@item.description</td>
            <td>@item.sellername</td>
            <td>@item.value</td>
            <td><button @onclick="@(async () => await
Delete(item.id))">Delete</button></td>
        </tr>
            }
        }
        else
        {
        }
    </tbody>
</table>
@code {
    List<DataModels.ProductModel> products;
```

```
    protected override async Task OnInitializedAsync()
    {
        products = await productmanagement.
GetAllProductsAsync();
    }
    async Task Delete(Guid id)
    {
        await productmanagement.DeleteProductAsync(id);
    }
}
```

As always, we first declare a route for the page, and in addition, we have an injection for our main service. The code section contains one variable, that is, the list of products. We retrieve and assign the list once, on the initialization of the page. Alternatively, you may have chosen to add a refresh button or simply have a button that fetches data without doing that on initialization. We also have a Delete method, which will delete the product. For the display, we first check if the list is assigned, and then we loop through each item by using the foreach loop. The items are displayed in table data cells, with the exception of the delete button. For the delete button, we establish an onclick event where we set our delete method and pass the ID for the current item.

Finally, we have two ways to navigate to our pages. The first and initial option is to use the links in the index (Listing 6-7), and the second option is to go through the nav bar (Listing 6-8).

Listing 6-7. Navigation Page

```
<div>
    <ul class="nav flex-column">
        <li class="nav-item px-3">
            <NavLink class="nav-link"
href="createproductpage" >
```

```
            <span class="oi oi-plus" aria--hidden="true">
Create product </span></NavLink>
      </li>
      <li class="nav-item px-3">
          <NavLink class="nav-link" href="viewproductspage">
              <span class="oi oi-home" aria--hidden="true">
Manage products</span>
          </NavLink>
      </li>
   </ul>
</div>
```

Listing 6-8. Index Page

```
@page "/"
<p><NavLink href="">Create product</NavLink></p>
<p><NavLink href="viewproductspage">View products</NavLink></p>
```

Task 2

This task will help you focus on component-based development. Rather than working with lots of pages, you will rely on components.

Description

Create a basketball game tracking application. This particular application will focus on you using Blazor, and you will explore how and why the server-side Blazor version would be useful for such a task.

Teams A and B are tracked separately; you should be able to register a statistics item by clicking a single button.

You will want to be able to register the following:

> Score 1 point
>
> Score 2 point
>
> Score 3 point
>
> Foul
>
> Rebound
>
> Block

You do not need to save anything, but do allow for that. Try to establish methods and structure for how you would save the data for the game.

Solution

Just like the first task and all the upcoming ones, this is not the only solution. But this is one of the more efficient ones. We will explore the general logic, as well as how you could go further if you actually needed to save those updates.

As you can see in Figure 6-2, there are only two pages: `Main.razor` and `TeamComponent.razor`. Also, the layout has been completely cleaned up, and we have only `@body` in it.

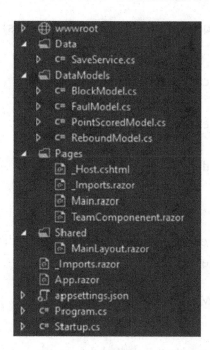

Figure 6-2. *Main.razor and TeamComponent.razor*

Listing 6-9. Point Model (PointModel.cs)

```
using System;
namespace WebApplication1.DataModels
{
    public class PointScoredModel
    {
      public  Guid id { get; set; }
      public  int value { get; set; }
    }
}
```

Listing 6-10. Rebound Model (ReboundModel.cs)

```
using System;
namespace WebApplication1.DataModels
{
    public class ReboundModel
    {
        public Guid id { get; set; }
    }
}
```

Listing 6-11 will be the model for a rebound record; this simply contains the ID for the record.

Listing 6-11. Foul Model (FoulModel.cs)

```
using System;
namespace WebApplication1.DataModels
{
    public class FoulModel
    {
        public Guid id { get; set; }
    }
}
```

Listing 6-12 will be the model for a foul record; like the previous one, this simply contains the ID for the record.

Listing 6-12. Block Model (BlockModel.cs)

```
using System;
namespace WebApplication1.DataModels
{
    public class BlockModel
```

```
    {
        public Guid id { get; set; }
    }
}
```

As you can see, for the most part, the models are quite straightforward (see Listings 6-9, 6-10, 6-11, and 6-12) with the exception of the score. Since we have three types of score (one point, two points, and three points), we could have three different models, but that would be inefficient and hard to read, and it would also present problems when displaying the total score for the team. If need be, you can always expand these models: add the time of the game, add the quarter, and add the player's number.

Listing 6-13. Main Page (Main.razor)

```
<p>Current score:
@{
    int currentscore = 0;
}
@foreach (var item in PointsList)
{
    currentscore += item.value;
}
    <label>@currentscore</label>
    </p>
<p>Total fouls: @FoulList.Count</p>
<p>Total rebounds: @ReboundList.Count</p>
<p>Total blocks: @BlockList.Count</p>
<p><button @onclick="@(() => AddPoint(1))">Add 1 pt
</button></p>
<p><button @onclick="@(() => AddPoint(2))">Add 2 pt
</button></p>
```

```
<p><button @onclick="@(() => AddPoint(3))">Add 3 pt
</button></p>
<p><button @onclick="@(() => AddFoul())">Add Foul</button></p>
<p><button @onclick="@(() => AddRebound())">Add rebound
</button></p>
<p><button @onclick="@(() => AddBlock())">Add block
</button></p>
@code {
    [Parameter]
    public int team { get; set; } = 1;// A - 1 or B - 2
    [Parameter]
    public Guid gameid { get; set; }
    List<DataModels.PointScoredModel> PointsList = new
List<DataModels.PointScoredModel>();
    List<DataModels.FoulModel> FoulList = new List<DataModels.
FoulModel>();
    List<DataModels.BlockModel> BlockList = new
List<DataModels.BlockModel>();
    List<DataModels.ReboundModel> ReboundList = new
List<DataModels.ReboundModel>();
    void AddPoint(int val)
    {
        PointsList.Add(new DataModels.PointScoredModel { id =
Guid.NewGuid(), value = val });
    }
    void AddFoul()
    {
        FoulList.Add(new DataModels.FoulModel() { id = Guid.
NewGuid() });
    }
    void AddBlock()
```

```
    {
        BlockList.Add(new DataModels.BlockModel() { id = Guid.
NewGuid() });
    }
    void AddRebound()
    {
        ReboundList.Add(new DataModels.ReboundModel() { id =
Guid.NewGuid() });
    }
}
```

As you saw in Figure 6-2, we have only one component for team data, and we have two teams. Therefore, we need to identify each component, and we do that by passing an integer as a parameter. We also pass the game ID as a parameter, where the ID will be generated in Main.razor. Going further with the variables, you can notice four lists were created, each with their own type of object. Also, you can see that we have only one list for the score, even though a score has three types. The types of score are declared as a value in the record. To display the current results, for the most part, we simply bind the Count property of Lists with the exception of the score. For the score, we are displaying the total; therefore, we need to calculate that. To make it simple, we just run a loop in the page, which gets rerun every time the Count property changes. Finally, we have a few methods that will simply add a new item on a click.

Listing 6-14. Index Page

```
@page "/"
<div style="width:50%;float:left;">
    <TeamComponenent team="1" gameid="@gameid">
</TeamComponenent>
</div>
<div style="width:50%;float:left;">
```

```
    <TeamComponenent team="2" gameid="@gameid" >
</TeamComponenent>
</div>
@code {
Guid gameid;
protected override Task OnInitializedAsync() {
    gameid = Guid.NewGuid();
    return base.OnInitializedAsync();
}
}
```

For our Main page, we have a default route declared, so it works like your generic Index.razor, except in this case, we have Main.razor. We also have our gameid variable declared, which is set on initialization, although you could simply set it on declaration. We also have two div elements, in which our team components are set. And as planned, we pass integers for each team; with that, we have gameid as well.

For the saving of records (Listing 6-15), we can elect to have a couple of options. If, say, you decide to include quarters and timer in general, you will probably want to save the whole thing after the end of some period of time. But if you want to be really safe, you will save on every action; therefore, you will need a method like SaveProgress_Blocks.

Listing 6-15. Service for Placeholder Methods (SaveService.cs)

```
using System;
using System.Collections.Generic;
using System.Threading.Tasks;
namespace WebApplication1.Data
{
    public class SaveService
    {
```

```
    public async Task SaveProgress(Guid gameid, int team,
    params object[] datatosave)
    {
    }
    public async Task SaveProgress_Score(Guid gameid,
    int team, List<DataModels.PointScoredModel> scores)
    {
    }
    public async Task SaveProgress_Fouls(Guid gameid,
    int team, List<DataModels.FoulModel> fouls)
    {
    }
    public async Task SaveProgress_Rebounds(Guid gameid,
    int team, List<DataModels.ReboundModel> rebounds)
    {
    }
    public async Task SaveProgress_Blocks(Guid gameid,
    int team, List<DataModels.BlockModel> blocks)
    {
    }
  }
}
```

Summary

As you can see, server-side Blazor is really convenient, but it is important not to forget that it uses lots of server resources. With that in mind, it is best used for tasks where the requirement is for data to reach the server frequently.

CHAPTER 7

Practice Tasks for Client-Side Blazor

You have already learned a lot from this book, but to truly learn, you have to practice. In this chapter, you will build a couple of projects.

Specifically, in this chapter, you will be able to practice the following:

- Blazor UI bindings

- Local storage in Blazor

- Event handling in Blazor

Task 1

Your first task will include several simple exercises to practice the general syntax of Blazor, as well as a more complex exercise where you will need to use components and local storage.

Description

You will create a Blazor client-side application that will allow you to make calculations according to the instructions provided. The application will include the following attributes:

- *Age calculator*: An age calculator simply allows you to enter two dates and return the difference in years.

- *Cylinder surface area*: Use the following formula:

  A = 2πrh + 2πr^2

where

  A = area

  r = radius

  h = height

This will allow you to calculate all the variables from the rest of them.

- *Rectangular area*: Use the following formula:

  A = a · b

where

  A = area

  a = side a

  b = side b

This will allow you to calculate all the variables from the rest of them. This app will allow the calculations to be saved locally for later use.

- *Trapezoid area calculator*: Use the following formula:

  A = (a + b) / 2 · h

where

  A = area

  a = base 1

  b = base 2

  h = height

This will allow you to calculate all the variables from the rest of them.

- *Area of triangle calculator*: Use the following formula:

$$A = (h \cdot b) / 2$$

where

A = area

h = height

b = base length

This will allow you to calculate all the variables from the rest of them.

- *Rectangular area calculator*: Use the following formula:

$$A = a \cdot b$$

where

A = area

a = side a

b = side b

This calculation is quite basic, but there is an additional task to go along with it. You will need to *locally save* each calculation if the user wants them to be saved. Then, the calculation history will be displayed in the page, and the user will be able to select one of them and insert the variable values from the record. Here are the extra steps:

1. Create calculator pages based on the formulas provided.

2. Add a local save feature for the calculation made for the rectangular area.

Solution

Our solution will be separated into several parts, for each part of description. As always, this is just one of many possible solutions rather than the only one.

Every calculation has its own page (see Figure 7-1), except for the rectangular calculation, where we also have a component for the history.

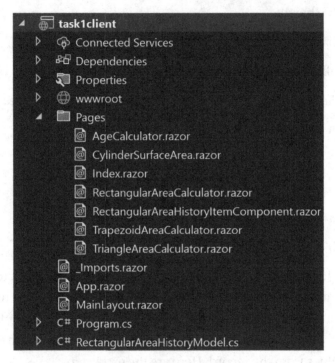

Figure 7-1. *Project structure for the solution*

Age Calculator Solution

Let's create the age calculator in this section.

As you can see, the age calculator is quite straightforward (see Listing 7-1); we simply have two variables of type datetime, and we bind them with the appropriate input fields.

Listing 7-1. Age Calculator Page

```
@page "/agecalculator"
<p>Birthdate: <input  @onchange="@((args) => { birthdate
= Convert.ToDateTime((string)args.Value); Calculate();
})"  type="date"/></p>
<p>To: <input @bind="@To"  type="date"/></p>
<p><button @onclick="@InsertToday">Insert today</button></p>
<p>Age: @age</p>
@code {
    DateTime birthdate = new DateTime(1965,12,15);
    DateTime To = DateTime.Now;
    double age;
    void InsertToday()
    {
        To = DateTime.Now;
    }
    void Calculate()
    {
        age = birthdate.Subtract(To).TotalDays / 365;
    }
}
```

The more interesting part of this is how we execute the `Calculate` method. The task does not have any specific requirements, but you can either create a simple button and execute it on a click/tap or do something more exciting like we have here. On a change of the value, we assign the new value to the variable, and with that, we also execute calculations. This is a good quick way to handle more than one operation in a single event.

Cylinder Surface Area Calculator

Let's look into calculating the surface area of cylinder in this section.
For the cylinder area calculator (Listing 7-2), we mostly have some basic
calculations being made.

Listing 7-2. Cylinder Surface Area Calculator Page

```
@page "/cylindersurfaceareacalculator"
<h3>Cylinder Surface Area Calculator</h3>
<p><input class="inputstyle"  @bind="@A" placeholder="A"/> =
2π * <input @bind="@r" class="inputstyle" placeholder="r"> *
<input @bind="@h" class="inputstyle" placeholder="h">
    + 2π * <input @bind="@r" class="inputstyle" placeholder="r" />
<sup>2</sup></p>
<p>A = 2πrh + 2πr<sup>2</sup></p>
<p>A - area <button @onclick="@Calculate_A">calculate A
</button></p>
<p>r - radius <button @onclick="@Calculate_r">calculate r
</button></p>
<p>π - @Math.PI</p>
<p>h - height <button @onclick="@Calculate_h">calculate h
</button></p>
@code {
    double r = 0;
    double h = 0;
    double A = 0;
    void Calculate_A()
    {
        A = 2 * Math.PI * r * h + 2 * Math.PI * Math.Pow(h,2);
    }
    void Calculate_r()
    {
```

```
    r = 0.5 * Math.Sqrt(Math.Pow(h, 2) + 2 * (A / Math.PI)) -
(h / 2);
    }
    void Calculate_h()
    {
        h = (A / (2 * Math.PI * r)) - r;
    }
}
```

The trick in this task is to put things in proper places and not make a mess of things, such as having the same formula for two different outputs. First, we display our formula in basic text format, and then we also have our formula with input fields in it. For each variable, we have different methods that calculate a value, and for each of them, we have different buttons that execute those methods.

Trapezoid Area Calculator

Let's look into calculating the area of trapezoid in this section. The trapezoid calculator will be similar to the one created in Listing 7-2. Again, the difficulty is not in finding something new, but rather in properly assigning all the variables where they fit (Listing 7-3).

Listing 7-3. Trapezoid Area Calculator Page

```
@page "/trapezoidareacalculator"
<p>@A = (<input @bind="@a"    class="inputstyle"
placeholder="a"/> +
    <input @bind="@b"    class="inputstyle" placeholder="b">) /
2 * <input @bind="@h"    class="inputstyle" placeholder="h"></p>
<p>A = (a + b) / 2 * h</p>
<p>A - area</p>
<p>a - base 1</p>
```

```
<p>b - base 2</p>
<p>h - height</p>
<p><button @onclick="@Calculate"></button></p>
@code {
    double A;
    double a;
    double b;
    double h;
    void Calculate()
    {
        A = (a + b) / 2 * h;
    }
}
```

Triangle Area Calculator

Let's look into calculating the area of triangle in this section. Our triangle calculation (Listing 7-4) is once again quite basic, and this is just one way to do it. You can, of course, do it on different events, or you may want to just display the output in a way where you would not have an interactive formula.

Listing 7-4. Triangle Area Calculator Page

```
@page "/triangleareacalculator"
    <p>
        <input class="inputstyle"
@bind="@A"   placeholder="A"> =
        (<input class="inputstyle" @bind="@h" placeholder="h">
* <input class="inputstyle" @bind="@b" placeholder="b">) / 2
    </p>
<p>A = (h * b) / 2</p>
<p>A - area <button @onclick="@Calculate_A">Calculate
</button></p>
```

```
<p>h - height <button @onclick="@Calculate_h">Calculate
</button></p>
<p>b - base length <button @onclick="@Calculate_b">Calculate
</button></p>
@code {
    double A;
    double h;
    double b;
    void Calculate_A()
    {
        A = (h * b) / 2;
    }
     void Calculate_h()
    {
        h = A * 2 / b;
    }
     void Calculate_b()
    {
        b = A * 2 / h;
    }
}
```

Rectangle Area Calculator

Let's look at calculating the area of a rectangle in this section (see Listing 7-5, 7-6). In this case, we can begin with setting up a data model for the results, as this will be used for both calculating and saving results. The result set contains data for all the variables in the calculation and the ID.

Listing 7-5. Calculation History Data Model

```
public class RectangularAreaHistoryModel
    {
        public string id { get; set; }
```

```
    public double A { get; set; }
    public double a { get; set; }
    public double b { get; set; }
}
```

Listing 7-6. Calculation History Item Component

```
<p>A: @item.A</p>
<p>side a: @item.a</p>
<p>side b: @item.b</p>
<p><button @onclick="@(async () => await OnSelect.
InvokeAsync(item.id))">Pick</button></p>
@code {
    [Parameter]
    public RectangularAreaHistoryModel item { get; set; }
    [Parameter]
    public EventCallback<string> OnSelect  { get; set; }
}
```

For the results, we have a component that will be displayed in a list. This simply takes a parameter for a record that will be displayed and a pick button that will invoke the OnSelect event, which will then trigger the display of those variables in the inputs for the calculator Listing 7-7.

Listing 7-7. Calculator Page

```
@page "/rectangulararecacalculator"
@inject IJSRuntime js
<p>
    <input @bind="@currentcalculation.A" class="inputstyle"
placeholder="A"> =
    <input @bind="@currentcalculation.a" class="inputstyle"
placeholder="a">
```

```
    *
    <input @bind="@currentcalculation.b" class="inputstyle"
placeholder="b">
</p>
<p>A = a * b</p>
<p>A - area <button @onclick="@Calculate_A">Calculate</
button></p>
<p>a - side a <button @onclick="@Calculate_a">Calculate</
button></p>
<p>b - side b <button @onclick="@Calculate_b">Calculate</
button></p>
<p style="color:red;">@error</p>
<p>Save calculations <input type="checkbox" @bind="@
savecalculation" /></p>
<p>History: </p>

@foreach (var item in calculationhistory)
{
    <RectangularAreaHistoryItemComponent  item="@item" OnSelect
="Selected"></RectangularAreaHistoryItemComponent>
}

@code {
    string error;

    List<RectangularAreaHistoryModel> calculationhistory = new
List<RectangularAreaHistoryModel>();
    bool savecalculation;
    RectangularAreaHistoryModel currentcalculation = new
RectangularAreaHistoryModel();

    async Task Calculate_A()
    {
```

```
        try
        {
            currentcalculation.A = currentcalculation.a *
currentcalculation.b;
            if (savecalculation)
            {
                await SaveCalculation();
            }
        }
        catch (Exception e)
        {
            error = "Something went wrong, try again";
        }
    }
    async Task Calculate_a()
    {
        try
        {
            currentcalculation.a = currentcalculation.A /
currentcalculation.b;
            if (savecalculation)
            {
                await  SaveCalculation();
            }
        }
        catch (Exception e)
        {
            error = "Something went wrong, try again";
        }

    }
    async Task Calculate_b()
```

```
    {
        try
        {
            currentcalculation.b = currentcalculation.A /
currentcalculation.a;
            if (savecalculation)
            {
                await SaveCalculation();
            }
        }
        catch (Exception e)
        {
            error = "Something went wrong, try again";
        }

    }
    async Task SaveCalculation()
    {
        try
        {

            currentcalculation.id = DateTime.UtcNow.Ticks.
ToString();

            calculationhistory.Add(currentcalculation);
            string json = System.Text.Json.JsonSerializer.
Serialize(calculationhistory);
            await js.InvokeAsync<object>("localStorage.
removeItem", "rectareacalculationhistory");
            await js.InvokeAsync<string>("localStorage.
setItem", "rectareacalculationhistory", json);
        }
```

```
        catch (Exception e)
        {
            error = "Something went wrong, try again" + e.Message;
        }

    }
    protected override async Task OnInitializedAsync()
    {
        try
        {
            string json = await js.InvokeAsync<string>("localSt
orage.getItem", "rectareacalculationhistory");

            calculationhistory = System.Text.Json.
JsonSerializer.Deserialize<List<RectangularAreaHistoryModel>>
(json);
        }
        catch (Exception e)
        {

        }

    }

    Task Selected(string id)
    {
        currentcalculation = calculationhistory.Find(x =>
x.id == id);

        return Task.CompletedTask;
    }
}
```

The calculation for rectangular variables is the same as others; we have variables set through input boxes, and then on submit the calculation is made based on formulas, in the methods Calculate_A, Calculate_b, and Calculate_a.

The difference here is that those methods also contain a check for a Boolean: savecalculation. It can be set to true or false using the checkbox, and if it is true, the calculation is saved. To save the calculation, the result data is serialized into a JSON string, which then is inserted into local storage. Notice that for the ID ticks of the current UTC date are used. Also, the ID can be reused as a date stamp for when the result was saved. Alternatively, the GUID could be used. Then, for reading the records, the system simply retrieves the JSON string from local storage and deserializes that to the result list.

Finally, since it suits us well, for the navigation we do not clear most of the defaults (see Listing 7-8); we just set up our navlinks according to the pages that we have. In real-world projects, it is a good idea to change the designs if you take this approach.

Listing 7-8. Navigation Page

```
<div class="top-row pl-4 navbar navbar-dark">
    <a class="navbar-brand" href="">BlazorApp1</a>
    <button class="navbar-toggler" @onclick="ToggleNavMenu">
        <span class="navbar-toggler-icon"></span>
    </button>
</div>
<div class="@NavMenuCssClass" @onclick="ToggleNavMenu">
    <ul class="nav flex-column">
        <li class="nav-item px-3">
            <NavLink class="nav-link" href=""
Match="NavLinkMatch.All">
```

```
                    <span class="oi oi-home" aria-hidden="true">
</span> Home
        </NavLink>
    </li>
    <li class="nav-item px-3">
        <NavLink class="nav-link" href="cylindersurfacearea
calculator">
            Cylinder surface area calculator
        </NavLink>
    </li>
    <li class="nav-item px-3">
        <NavLink class="nav-link"
href="triangleareacalculator">
            triangle area calculator
        </NavLink>
    </li>
    <li class="nav-item px-3">
        <NavLink class="nav-link" href="agecalculator">
            age calculator
        </NavLink>
    </li>
    <li class="nav-item px-3">
        <NavLink class="nav-link" href="rectangulararea
calculator">
            Rectangle area calculator
        </NavLink>
    </li>
    <li class="nav-item px-3">
        <NavLink class="nav-link" href="trapezoidarea
calculator">
            trapezoid area calculator
```

```
            </NavLink>
        </li>
    </ul>
</div>
@code {
    bool collapseNavMenu = true;
    string NavMenuCssClass => collapseNavMenu ?
"collapse" : null;
    void ToggleNavMenu()
    {
        collapseNavMenu = !collapseNavMenu;
    }
}
```

Task 2

For this task, we'll build an invoice generator. The invoice is basically a written request from one business to another for a payment. The invoice generator should state the company details, items, values, and total values. Our version will be simplified.

Description

Since our invoice is simplified, we will have only a couple of company details, and the biggest part of the development will be a sales item. The user should be able to add as many items as they want, and the total each time should be added to the total of the invoice.

Here are the inputs:

- ID

- Description

- Total (generated from items)

117

Here are the sales items:

- Description
- Price
- Tax
- Total

In the sales items, you also need to provide the total for each item. Use a component for a sales item. Note that you are not required to do any actual PDF, PNG, or other visual outputs of the invoice.

Solution

Just like the previous task, this is not the only solution possible, but your project will be similar.

Since we need only one page for this application, we will not have too many files; rather, we will work on the index page and create a single component for a sales item, which we will explore later. The layout is also basic (Listing 7-9 and Figure 7-2); we have removed all the default stuff and left just a skeleton layout.

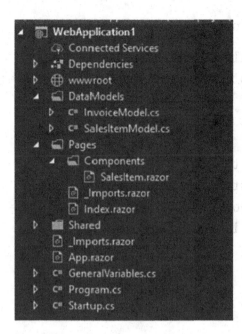

Figure 7-2. *Project structure for the solution*

Listing 7-9. Main Layout

```
@inherits LayoutComponentBase
    <div style="width:100%;float:left;">
        @Body
    </div>
```

For our invoice, we need to create a couple of data models (see Listings 7-10 and 7-11). While the task does not require us to generate the files, we still want to prepare for that. The invoice simply contains an ID, description, total, and then the sales items added to it. The sales item is quite basic as well; we have an item ID, description, price, tax, and total. Everything here is very generic, and the interesting part will begin in the index page.

Listing 7-10. Invoice Model (InvoiceModel.cs)

```
using System.Collections.Generic;
namespace WebApplication1.DataModels
{
    public class InvoiceModel
    {
        public string id { get; set; }
        public string description { get; set; }
        public double total { get; set; }
        public List<SalesItemModel> salesitems
        {
            get;  set;
        }
    }
}
```

Listing 7-11. Sales Item Model (SalesItemModel.cs)

```
namespace WebApplication1.DataModels
{
    public class SalesItemModel
    {
        public string itemid { get; set; }
        public string description { get; set; }
        public double price { get; set; } = 0;
        public double tax { get; set; } = 0;
        public double total { get; set; } = 0;
    }
}
```

Listing 7-12. Main Page (Index.razor)

```
@page "/"
@inject IJSRuntime js
    <div style="float:left;width:100%;">
        <p>Total: @total</p>
        <p>Total tax: @totaltax</p>
        <p>Description</p>
        <p><textarea @bind="@currentinvoice.description">
</textarea></p>
        <p>Sales items</p>
        <p><button @onclick="@AddNewItem">Add</button></p>
    </div>
@foreach (var item in currentinvoice.salesitems)
{
    <WebApplication1.Pages.Components.SalesItem
OnDescription Change="ChangeForItemDescription" OnValueChan
ge="ChangeForItemValue" OnTotalChange="ChangeForItemTotal"
OnTaxChange="ChangeForItemTax" OnRemove="RemoveItem"
@key="item.itemid" _itemid="@item.itemid"></WebApplication1.
Pages.Components.SalesItem>
}
@code {
    DataModels.InvoiceModel currentinvoice = new DataModels.
InvoiceModel() { id = Guid.NewGuid().ToString(), salesitems =
new List<DataModels.SalesItemModel>() };
    double total = 0;
    double totaltax = 0;
    void AddNewItem()
    {
        currentinvoice.salesitems.Add(new DataModels.
SalesItemModel() { itemid = Guid.NewGuid().ToString() });
```

```
    }
    void RemoveItem( string id)
    {
        currentinvoice.salesitems.Remove(currentinvoice.
salesitems.Where(x => x.itemid == id).ToArray()[0]);
    }
    void ChangeForItemDescription(KeyValuePair<string,str
ing> args)
    {
        currentinvoice.salesitems.Find(x => x.itemid == args.
Key).description = args.Value;
    }
    void ChangeForItemValue(KeyValuePair<string,double> args)
    {
        currentinvoice.salesitems.Find(x => x.itemid == args.
Key).price = args.Value;
    }
    void ChangeForItemTax(KeyValuePair<string,double> args)
    {
        currentinvoice.salesitems.Find(x => x.itemid == args.
Key).tax = args.Value;
        totaltax = 0;
        foreach (var item in currentinvoice.salesitems)
        {
            totaltax += item.tax;
        }
    }
    void ChangeForItemTotal(KeyValuePair<string,double> args)
    {
        currentinvoice.salesitems.Find(x => x.itemid == args.
Key).total = args.Value;
```

```
        total = 0;
        foreach (var item in currentinvoice.salesitems)
        {
            total += item.total;
        }
    }
}
```

Listing 7-13. Sales Item Component (SalesItem.razor)

```
<div style="float:left;width:100%;">
    <p><button @onclick="@(async () => await OnRemove.
InvokeAsync(_itemid))">Remove</button></p>
    <p>description:</p>
    <p><input @onchange="@(async (args) => await
OnDescriptionChange.InvokeAsync(new KeyValuePair<string,
string>(_itemid, (string)args.Value)))"></p>
    <p>value:</p>
    <p><input  @onchange="@((args) =>  ReeveluateAfterValueChange
(Convert.ToDouble(args.Value)))" ></p>
    <p>tax:</p>
    <p><input @onchange="@((args)
=>  ReeveluateAfterTaxChange(Convert.ToDouble(args.
Value)))" ></p>
    <p>total:</p>
    <p>@total</p>
    <p>@_itemid</p>
</div>
@code  {
    [Parameter]
    public string _itemid { get; set; }
    [Parameter]
```

```
    public EventCallback<string> OnRemove { get; set; }
    [Parameter]
    public EventCallback<KeyValuePair<string,string>>
OnDescriptionChange { get; set; }
    [Parameter]
    public EventCallback<KeyValuePair<string,double>>
OnValueChange { get; set; }
    [Parameter]
    public EventCallback<KeyValuePair<string,double>>
OnTaxChange { get; set; }
    [Parameter]
    public EventCallback<KeyValuePair<string,double>>
OnTotalChange { get; set; }
    double total;
    double value;
    double tax;
    async void ReeveluateAfterValueChange(double newvalue)
    {
        value = newvalue;
        await OnValueChange.InvokeAsync(new
KeyValuePair<string, double>(_itemid,value));
        total = value + (tax / 100) * value;
        await OnTotalChange.InvokeAsync(new
KeyValuePair<string, double>(_itemid, total));
    }
     async void ReeveluateAfterTaxChange(double newvalue)
    {
        tax = newvalue;
        await OnValueChange.InvokeAsync(new
KeyValuePair<string, double>(_itemid,value));
        total = value + (tax / 100) * value;
```

```
        await OnTotalChange.InvokeAsync(new
KeyValuePair<string, double>(_itemid, total));
    }
}
```

While the invoice page and items component may seem complex, when you look closely, they use only the most basic features of Blazor. The most difficult part here is dealing with the components and attempting to calculate the total when there are changes. The component (Listing 7-13) simply takes an ID, because when it gets generated, all the values are empty. The most important parts here are the callbacks; as you can see, all the input fields have one, and they all act differently. The description is the simplest one, as it only returns the ID and the new description value. The tax and value are more complex; we first need to establish methods, which will calculate the values in the component and display them in the component directly. Then, these methods invoke our callbacks; to get further, we need to switch to the page. Our page (shown in Listing 7-12) handles the callbacks differently, but for the most part, the idea is to assign the values to the list of items, because that is what would be generated for some kind of visual format.

Summary

Both of these tasks not only give you an opportunity to practice your skills but also showed you how client-side Blazor can make your business more efficient. For any of these tasks, there is absolutely no need to go to the server side, which saves you a lot of money. Using components simplifies development and keeps your code cleaner.

CHAPTER 8

Practice Tasks for the Blazor Hosted Version

In this chapter, you will continue practicing what you have learned previously, but there will be only one project to complete. At this point, you should be comfortable with client-side development, but a little more practice will not hurt.

In this chapter, you will be able to practice the following:

- Project setup for the Blazor hosted version
- Blazor bindings
- Blazor method executions
- API calls in Blazor
- Downloading files in Blazor

Task 1

For your Blazor hosted task, you will need to create a program that deals with the statistics of poker players. During this task, you will notice how easy it is to use the shared data model feature, as well as how useful it is to have a client-side file generation capability.

© Taurius Litvinavicius 2023

T. Litvinavicius, *Exploring Blazor*, https://doi.org/10.1007/978-1-4842-8768-2_8

Description

You will need to first display a list of players, for which you can simply use a button containing the name of the player. On the selection (click) of the player, their statistics will be fetched and displayed. The statistics data for each player will be cached, meaning that if the player is selected again, after another one has been selected, the data will not be retrieved from the server unless the user refreshes it. The next part of the task is for the client side; the program should allow you to export a JSON file of selected player statistics or the statistics for all cached players.

Here is the player statistics output:

- Total tournaments

- Total winnings

- Tournaments in the money

- Date started

- Last updated (either retrieved or refreshed)

Resources

You will be provided with a class that contains a list of users and two methods that will retrieve both the list and the statistics for each player.

First, we have our PlayerData model (see Listing 8-1), which will be our main model in this fake database. It will also create a static list, with some items for you to work with. You will only need to deal with the following methods:

- RetrievePlayerList: Fetches the list of players, but takes and gives only an ID and a name for each player

- RetrievePlayerStatistics: Fetches the full details for a single player

Listing 8-1. Players.cs

```
using System;
using System.Collections.Generic;
using System.Linq;
using System.Threading.Tasks;
namespace Task1.Server.DataLogic
{
    public class Players
    {
        static List<PlayerData> PlayersList = new
        List<PlayerData>() {
            new PlayerData
            {
                id = 1,
                name = "John dow",
                totaltournaments = 1100,
                totalwinnings = 115000,
                totalinthemoney = 250,
                datestarted = DateTime.Parse("08/20/2005")
            },
             new PlayerData
            {
                id = 2,
                name = "John mark",
                totaltournaments = 1500,
                totalwinnings = 15005,
                totalinthemoney = 15,
                datestarted = DateTime.Parse("02/25/2009")
            },
```

```
        new PlayerData
    {
        id = 3,
        name = "John dean",
        totaltournaments = 1300,
        totalwinnings = 134000,
        totalinthemoney = 468,
        datestarted = DateTime.Parse("12/25/2017")
    },
        new PlayerData
    {
        id = 4,
        name = "mark lee",
        totaltournaments = 150,
        totalwinnings = 5300,
        totalinthemoney = 7,
        datestarted = DateTime.Parse("06/25/2008")
    },
        new PlayerData
    {
        id = 5,
        name = "t young",
        totaltournaments = 101,
        totalwinnings = 18000,
        totalinthemoney = 19,
        datestarted = DateTime.Parse("08/25/2013")
    },
        new PlayerData
    {
        id = 6,
        name = "richar right",
```

```
            totaltournaments = 36,
            totalwinnings = 1300000,
            totalinthemoney = 10,
            datestarted = DateTime.Parse("08/25/1995")
        }
    };
    class PlayerData
    {
        public int id { get; set; }
        public string name { get; set; }
        public int totaltournaments { get; set; }
        public double totalwinnings { get; set; }
        public double totalinthemoney { get; set; }
        public DateTime datestarted { get; set; }
    }
    public static    Task<List<Shared.PlayerListItem>>
    RetrievePlayerList()
    {
        List<Shared.PlayerListItem> templist = new
        List<Shared.PlayerListItem>();
        foreach (var item in PlayersList)
        {
            templist.Add(new Shared.PlayerListItem()
            { id = item.id, name = item.name });
        }
        return Task.FromResult(templist);
    }
```

```
public static Task<Shared.PlayerStatisticsItem>
RetrievePlayerStatistics(int id)
{
    var selectedplayer = PlayersList.Where(cl => cl.id
    == id).ElementAt(0);
    return Task.FromResult(new Shared.
    PlayerStatisticsItem() {
        playerid = id,
        totaltournaments = selectedplayer.
        totaltournaments,
        totalinthemoney = selectedplayer.
        totalinthemoney,
        totalwinnings = selectedplayer.totalwinnings,
        datestarted = selectedplayer.datestarted,
        lastrefresh = DateTime.UtcNow
    });
}
    }
}
```

Solution

Now that you have your task completed, you can take a look at one
solution. As long as it is working, it is probably right, but there are many
ways to do it, and some ways might be more efficient than others.

First, we should start from the data models (see Figure 8-1) and then
move to the back end. For this application, we will need only two models:
one for the listing (Listing 8-2) and the other one for the statistics (Listing 8-3)
of the user. As you can see, these do not contain all the user data, only what
you need to display.

Figure 8-1. *Shared library*

Listing 8-2. Player List Item Model (PlayerListItem.cs)

```
namespace Task1.Shared
{
    public  class PlayerListItem
    {
        public string name { get; set; }
        public int id { get; set; }
    }
}
```

Listing 8-3. Player Statistics Item Model (PlayerStatisticsItem.cs)

```
using System;
namespace Task1.Shared
{
    public class PlayerStatisticsItem
    {
        public int playerid { get; set; }
        public int totaltournaments { get; set; }
        public double totalwinnings { get; set; }
        public double totalinthemoney { get; set; }
        public DateTime datestarted { get; set; }
        public DateTime lastrefresh { get; set; }
    }
}
```

Now that we have all that, we can move on to the server part (Figure 8-2).

Figure 8-2. *API project in the solution*

First, we need to create a `Player.cs` class, where we simply insert the contents provided in the resources. The file is conveniently placed in the `DataLogic` folder, which in this structure would contain only the classes that have methods for data retrieval, insertion, or other database-related procedures. Then, we can move on to the controller (Listing 8-4) where we have two routes: for the list and for the statistics.

Listing 8-4. Players Controller (PlayerController.cs)

```
using System.Collections.Generic;
using System.Threading.Tasks;
using Microsoft.AspNetCore.Mvc;
namespace WebApplication1.Server.Controllers
{
    public class PlayersController : Controller
    {
      [Route("/retrieveplayerslist")]
      [HttpGet]
```

```
public async Task<List<Shared.
PlayerListItem>> GetPlayers()
{
    return await DataLogic.Players.
    RetrievePlayerList();
}
[Route("/retrieveplayerstats")]
[HttpGet]
public async Task<Shared.PlayerStatisticsItem>
GetPlayerStats(int id)
{
    return await DataLogic.Players.
    RetrievePlayerStatistics(id);
}
    }
}
```

As you can see, the action methods execute only the static methods from the data logic; this helps to keep the controller completely clean.

Everything related to the client side (Figure 8-3) will be done in a single page (Index.razor in this case). However, you may have chosen to use components that would have made the page look cleaner, although it would have taken more time to set up.

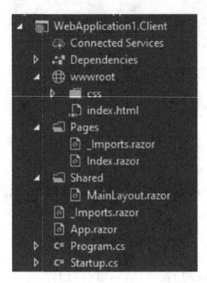

Figure 8-3. *Client project in the solution*

First, we need to establish some general declarations (Listing 8-5), starting with the page route. With the route, we need to declare a `using` statement for the shared folder; since we already have a namespace `Shared` in the client part, we elect to use a name for the namespace `Task1.Shared: datamodels`. We will be using Newtonsoft for our JSON exports; therefore, it is convenient to declare the `Newtonsoft.Json` namespace. Finally, we have two injections: one for the HTTP client, which will be used in API calls, and the other for IJSRuntime, which we will use to save the file.

Listing 8-5. Main Page (Index.razor)

```
@page "/"
```

<PlayerStatisticsComponent></PlayerStatisticsComponent>

We start the `Index.razor` page (Listing 8-6) by declaring two variables that will be used to display outputs. The first one is the list `listofplayers`; this will hold the list objects where we find the name and ID. The method

FetchPlayers will retrieve players from the server and assign them to the list. After that, the list is displayed in the first div element. Here we first check if the list contains any items; if not, we simply tell the user that the system has no players to display. On the other hand, if the list is filled, we will go through each item and assign the values to the button text (name), and in the onclick for the button, we will pass a parameter (id) to the method ShowPlayerStatistics. This method will retrieve the statistics data for that specific user from the server, but before that, we will try to check our dictionary PlayerStatisticsCache to see if the player statistics have already been cached; if they have, we will simply assign them to the CurrentPlayerDisplayed variable, and if not, we will retrieve the data and assign the statistics. Once they are assigned, the if statement is re-evaluated, and the variables in the object are updated in all the necessary places.

Listing 8-6. Player Statistics Component
(PlayerStatisticsComponent.razor)

```
@inject HttpClient http
@inject IJSRuntime jsruntime

<div>
        <p><button @onclick="@(async () => await
FetchPlayers())">Fetch players</button></p>
        @if (listofplayers.Count > 0)
        {
            foreach (var item in listofplayers)
            {
                <p><button @onclick="@(async () => await
                ShowPlayerStatistics(item.id))">@item.name
                </button></p>
            }
        }
```

```
        else
        {
            <p>No players available</p>
        }
    </div>
    <div>
        @if (CurrentPlayerDisplayed != null)
        {
            <p>total tournaments played:
            @CurrentPlayerDisplayed.totaltournaments</p>
            <p>total winnings: @CurrentPlayerDisplayed.
            totalwinnings</p>
            <p>total in the money: @CurrentPlayerDisplayed.
            totalinthemoney</p>
            <p>date started: @CurrentPlayerDisplayed.
            datestarted.ToShortDateString()</p>
            <p>Last refreshed: @(Math.Ceiling
            (CurrentPlayerDisplayed.lastrefresh.
            Subtract(DateTime.UtcNow).TotalMinutes))
            minutes ago</p>
            <p><button @onclick="@(async () => await Ref
            reshPlayerStatistics(CurrentPlayerDisplayed.
            playerid))">Refresh</button></p>
            <p><button @onclick="@(async () => await
            ExportCurrentPlayer())">Export player</button></p>
        }
        else
        {
            <p  >Select a player for display</p>
        }
    </div>
<div>
```

```
<p><button @onclick="@(async () => await
ExportAllPlayers())" >Export all players</button></p>
</div>
@code    {
    List<Task1.Shared.PlayerListItem> listofplayers = new
    List<Task1.Shared.PlayerListItem>();
    Dictionary<int, Task1.Shared.PlayerStatisticsItem>
    PlayerStatisticsCache = new Dictionary<int, Task1.Shared.
    PlayerStatisticsItem>();
    Task1.Shared.PlayerStatisticsItem
    CurrentPlayerDisplayed = null;
    async Task FetchPlayers()
    {
        listofplayers = await http.GetFromJsonAsync<List<Task1.
        Shared.PlayerListItem>>("/retrieveplayerslist");
    }
    async Task ShowPlayerStatistics(int id)
    {
        bool iscached = PlayerStatisticsCache.TryGetValue(id,
        out CurrentPlayerDisplayed);
        if (!iscached)
        {
            CurrentPlayerDisplayed = await http.
            GetFromJsonAsync<Task1.Shared.PlayerStatisticsItem>
            ("/retrieveplayerstats?id="+id);
            PlayerStatisticsCache.Add(id,
            CurrentPlayerDisplayed);
        }
    }
    async Task RefreshPlayerStatistics(int id)
    {
```

```
            CurrentPlayerDisplayed = await
            http.GetFromJsonAsync<Task1.
            Shared.PlayerStatisticsItem>("/
            retrieveplayerstats?id="+id);
            PlayerStatisticsCache[id] = CurrentPlayerDisplayed;
    }
    async Task ExportCurrentPlayer()
    {

        string json = System.Text.Json.JsonSerializer.Serialize
        (CurrentPlayerDisplayed);
        string base64 = Convert.ToBase64String(System.Text.
        Encoding.UTF8.GetBytes(json));
        await jsruntime.InvokeAsync<object>("downloadfile",
        "PlayerStats_" + DateTime.UtcNow.ToFileTimeUtc().
        ToString() + ".json",base64);
    }
    async Task ExportAllPlayers()
    {

        string json = System.Text.Json.JsonSerializer.Serialize
        (PlayerStatisticsCache);
        string base64 = Convert.ToBase64String(System.Text.
        Encoding.UTF8.GetBytes(json));
        await jsruntime.InvokeAsync<object>("downloadfile",
        "AllPlayers_" + DateTime.UtcNow.ToFileTimeUtc().
        ToString() + ".json",base64);
    }
}
```

For the exporting part, we will need to use a bit of JavaScript just
to establish one function (Listing 8-7), which will "download" the
file from the client side. Then, to export a single player, we will use
ExportCurrentPlayer, which serializes the CurrentPlayerDisplayed

variable to a JSON string, then converts a string to a byte array, and finally converts that to a base64 string. Once we have a base64 string, we can pass it to the JavaScript along with the name for the file.

Listing 8-7. File Download Script (JavaScript)

```javascript
function downloadfile(name, bt64) {
    var downloadlink = document.createElement('a');
    downloadlink.download = name;
    downloadlink.href = "data:application/octet-
    stream;base64," + bt64;
    document.body.appendChild(downloadlink);
    downloadlink.click();
    document.body.removeChild(downloadlink);
        }
```

Exporting all players would use the method `ExportAllPlayers`, and it would work in the same way, except it would use the `PlayerStatisticsCache` variable.

Summary

As you probably have noticed throughout this project, merging the API and client-side solutions is efficient, mainly because of the shared models' libraries. The testing is also a bit easier, as you do not need to launch two projects at the same time. With all the knowledge that you have acquired and the practice that you have done, you should be able to develop real-world projects now.

Index

A

Age calculator, 104, 105

B

Background tasks, 75, 76
Binding variables, 10
Blazor
  buttons and C# code, 53
  client-side version, 5
  client type, 3, 4
  C# method, 59
  interaction with
    JavaScript, 57, 58
  layouts, 31–33
  libraries, 71
  Razor syntax, 2
  server-side type, 3
  technical aspects, 2
  web applications
    development, 1
  WebSocket, 2
  web UI framework, 1
Blazor binds
  elements, 11–13
  event argument, 16, 17
  events, 13–16
  page/component cycle, 17, 18

Blazor Client-Side (WebAssembly)
  Template
  calling APIs, 42, 44, 50
  data class model, 49, 51, 52
  _Host.cshtml file, 37, 38
  JavaScript and CSS files, 39
Blazor code library project, 72–74
Blazor hosted task, 45
  client-side file generation
    capability, 128
  description, 128
  resources, 128, 129
  solution, 132–141
Blazor libraries, 34
Blazor navigation, 37
Blazor-related services, 36
Blazor server app, 35
Blazor server app empty, 36
Blazor server-side template
  adding API controllers, 44, 45
  Blazor server app, 35, 36
  data model class, 48
  default files, 36
  fallback page, 37
  interface part, 48
  one-project arrangement, 46, 47
  static values, 41
  WebSocket, 36
Blazor-specific techniques, 22

Printed in the United States
by Baker & Taylor Publisher Services